# The AA POCKETGuide
# CRETE

D1393250

**Crete:** Regions and Best places to see

★ Best places to see 20–41

■ Featured sight

Iráklio Province 45–63

Rethymno Province 90–103

Lasithiou Province 64–89

Hania Province 104–127

**Original text by Susie Boulton**
Updated by Mike Gerrard

© Automobile Association Developments Limited 2008. First published 2008

ISBN: 978-0-7495-5753-9

Published by AA Publishing, a trading name of Automobile Association Developments
Limited, whose registered office is Fanum House, Basing View, Basingstoke,
Hampshire RG21 4EA. Registered number 1878835.

Colour separation: Keenes, Andover
Printed and bound in Italy by Printer Trento S.r.l.

Front cover images: (t) AA/K Paterson; (b) AA/K Paterson
Back cover image: AA/P Enticknap

A03604
Maps in this title produced from mapping © Freytag-Berndt u.Artaria KG, 1231
Vienna-Austria

# About this book

**Symbols are used to denote the following categories:**

➕ map reference to maps

✉ address or location

☎ telephone number

🕐 opening times

✋ admission charge

🍴 restaurant or café on premises or nearby

Ⓜ nearest underground train station

🚌 nearest bus/tram route

🚆 nearest overground train station

⛴ nearest ferry stop

✈ nearest airport

❓ other practical information

ℹ tourist information office

➤ indicates the page where you will find a fuller description

This book is divided into four sections.

**Planning** pages 6–19
Before you go; Getting there; Getting around; Being there

**Best places to see** pages 20–41
The unmissable highlights of any visit to Crete

**Exploring** pages 42–127
The best places to visit in Crete, organized by area

**Maps** pages 131–142
All map references are to the maps on the covers. For example, Malia has the reference ➕ 137 B8 – indicating the page number and grid square in which it can be found

# Contents

INDEX & ACKNOWLEDGEMENTS

MAPS

131 – 142

# Planning

# Before you go

## WHEN TO GO

| JAN | FEB | MAR | APR | MAY | JUN | JUL | AUG | SEP | OCT | NOV | DEC |
|-----|-----|-----|-----|-----|-----|-----|-----|-----|-----|-----|-----|
| 12°C | 12°C | 14°C | 17°C | 20°C | 24°C | 26°C | 26°C | 24°C | 21°C | 17°C | 14°C |
| 54°F | 54°F | 57°F | 63°F | 68°F | 75°F | 79°F | 79°F | 75°F | 70°F | 63°F | 57°F |

🌧 High season  🌧 Low season

Crete is not quite an all-year destination, as winters can be cold and wet although they will also have their spells of lovely, mild, sunny weather. As Crete is not too far from north Africa it isn't surprising that summers can be very hot, especially in the south of the island.

Crete has a slightly longer and drier season than Greek islands further north, but you can't rule out rain and cold weather at either end of the summer season, in March/April and September/October.

The island is probably at its most beautiful in April/May, when the winter rains ought to have receded and the spring flowers are in full bloom, especially in the mountains. It is the perfect time for enjoying what Crete has to offer away from the beaches.

## WHAT YOU NEED

● Required
○ Suggested
▲ Not required

Some countries require a passport to remain valid for a minimum period (usually at least six months) beyond the date of entry – contact their consulate or embassy or your travel agency for details.

| | UK | Germany | USA | Netherlands | Spain |
|---|---|---|---|---|---|
| Passport/National Identity Card | ● | ● | ● | ● | ● |
| Visa (regulations can change – check before booking your trip) | ▲ | ▲ | ▲ | ▲ | ▲ |
| Onward or Return Ticket | ▲ | ▲ | ▲ | ▲ | ▲ |
| Health Inoculations | ○ | ○ | ○ | ○ | ○ |
| Health Documentation (▶ 9, Health Insurance) | ● | ● | ▲ | ● | ● |
| Travel Insurance | ● | ● | ● | ● | ● |
| Driving Licence (National or International) | ● | ● | ● | ● | ● |
| Car Insurance Certificate (if own car) | ● | ● | ● | ● | ● |
| Car Registration Document (if own car) | ● | ● | ● | ● | ● |

## WEBSITES

The official websites are:
www.greektourism.com;
www.gnto.co.uk

Visitors may also find the
following useful:
www.explorecrete.com
www.crete.tournet.gr

## TOURIST OFFICES AT HOME

### In the UK

Greek National Tourist Organisation
(GNTO/EOT)
4 Conduit Street,
London W1R ODJ
☎ 020 7495 9300

### In the USA

GNTO/EOT
Olympic Tower

645 Fifth Avenue
New York, NY 10022
☎ 212/ 421-5777

### In Canada

GNTO/EOT
1170 Place du Frère André
Suite 300, Montréal, Quebec
H3B 3C6
☎ 514/871-1535

## HEALTH INSURANCE

Visitors from the European Union (EU) are entitled to reciprocal state
medical care in Greece and should take with them a European Health
Insurance Card (EHIC), applications are available from post offices, or
apply online. However, private medical insurance is also recommended.

Dental treatment must be paid for by all visitors. Hotels can usually
provide names of local English-speaking dentists; or ask your Consulate.
Private medical insurance is strongly advised for dental treatment.

## TIME DIFFERENCES

| GMT | Crete | Germany | USA (NY) | Netherlands | Spain |
| 12 noon | 2PM | 1PM | 7AM | 1PM | 1PM |

Crete is two hours ahead of Greenwich Mean Time (GMT + 2). The clocks
go forward one hour on the last Sunday in March and back one hour on
the last Sunday in October.

## NATIONAL HOLIDAYS

| | | |
|---|---|---|
| 1 Jan *New Year's Day* | 1 May *Labour Day* | 26 Dec *St Stephen's Day* |
| 6 Jan *Epiphany* | May/Jun *Ascension Day* | |
| Feb/Mar *'Clean Monday'* | 15 Aug *Feast of the* | Restaurants and some |
| 25 Mar *Independence Day* | *Assumption* | tourists shops may stay |
| Mar/Apr *Good Friday and* | 28 Oct *Óchi Day* | open on these days, but |
| *Easter Monday* | 25 Dec *Christmas Day* | museums will be closed. |

## WHAT'S ON WHEN
### Festivals

The Greeks have a passion for festivals and fairs, and the Cretans are no exception. Villages celebrate their saint's name day with parades, fireworks, singing and dancing. While some of the island's festivals are strictly religious, others are aimed primarily at tourists. Either way the celebrations are very colourful events.

**January** *New Year's Day* (1 Jan): processions, traditional seasonal songs and cutting of the New Year's Cake to find the lucky coin.
*Epiphany* (6 Jan): blessings of the water; crosses thrown into the sea.

**March** *Katharí Deftéri 'Clean Monday'* (last Monday before Lent): celebrations marking the end of Carnival and beginning of Lent.
*Independence Day* (25 Mar): military parades.
*Holy Week.* Greek Orthodox Easter falls up to four weeks either side of the Western festival. This is the most important religious festival in Greece, celebrated with church services, processions, dancing, singing, feasting and fireworks.

**May** *Labour Day* (1 May): parades and flower festivals.
*Commemorations of the Battle of Crete* (late May), celebrated in Hania.

**July** There are festivals and folk performances all over Crete during the busy summer season. Local tourist offices can provide you with information. Iráklio has a summer festival of music, opera, drama, ballet, dancing and jazz.
*Cretan Wine Festival* (late Jul): a week of wine tasting and dancing in Rethymno.

**August** *Feast of the Metamorphosis* (6 Aug).

*Sultana Festival* (mid-Aug), in Sitia.
*Feast of the Assumption* (15 Aug). Pilgrimage for those named Ioánnis (John) to the Church of Agios Ioánnis on the Rodopou peninsula, Hania (29 Aug).
*Summer in Hania*: music, dance, shows.
*Renaissance Festival*: music, drama and films at the Venetian fortress in Rethymno.

**October** *Chestnut Festival* (mid-Oct), in Élos and other villages of southwest Crete.
*Óchi Day* ('No' Day, 28 Oct): commemorating the day the Greeks turned down Mussolini's ultimatum in World War II.

**November** Commemoration in Rethymno and Arkádi of the destruction of the Arkádi monastery in 1866 by the Turks (7–9 Nov).
*Feast of the Presentation of the Virgin in the Temple* (21 Nov), in Rethymno.

**December** *Christmas Day* (25 Dec): a feast day, but less significant to the Cretans than Easter.
*St Stephen's Day* (26 Dec).

# Getting there

## BY AIR

**Iráklio Airport**

5km (3 miles) to city centre

🚊 N/A

🚌 15 minutes

🚗 10 minutes

**Hania Airport**

12km (7.5 miles) to city centre

🚊 N/A

🚌 20 minutes

🚗 15 minutes

The majority of direct flights to Crete are charters from major European cities, available only from about Easter to October. Tour operators fly mainly to Iráklio, though some also use Hania airport for resorts in western Crete. There has been talk of developing the airport in Sitia for eastern Crete for the last few years, but this has been close to materialise. There are scheduled flights to Athens from Europe and the USA, with connections to Crete.

# Getting around

## BY AIR

If travelling within Greece there are a number of smaller airlines as well as the national carrier, Olympic. These include Aegean Airlines and Sky Express, the latter based on Crete. Sky Express has year-round flights to Crete from other Greek islands including Rhodes, Lesbos and Samos, and an increased service, including to Santorini, in summer.

## BY FERRY

There are several ferries per day, or overnight, from the Athens port of Piraeus to Iráklio, Hania and Rethymno. Some are much faster than others, so check sailing times first. There are also slightly less frequent sailings to Agios Nikolaos and Sitia. If you want to take your car to Crete it almost inevitably means going through Athens first and taking a car ferry from there.

## PUBLIC TRANSPORT

**Buses**  Crete has an extensive network of buses, providing a cheap and reasonably reliable service throughout the island. There is an excellent service along the main highway linking Agios Nikolaos, Iráklio, Rethymno and Hania, with buses at least every hour. From these towns there are services to smaller towns and most villages. Iráklio has three bus stations, operating services to different regions. Only buses within Iráklio are numbered – others show the destination (not always the right one) on the front of the bus. Local bus timetables are available from bus stations, local tourist offices and sometimes at bus stops. You need to flag down the bus as it approaches.

Timetables are available at main bus stations, or perhaps pinned to a tree or in the café window in remoter villages. Services are operated by the KTEL company, and they have comprehensive timetables and maps on their website: www.bus-service-crete-ktel.com.

**Ferries and boat trips**  Ferries connect Iráklio, Hania and Agios Nikolaos with the mainland at Piraeus and with other islands such as Rhodes and Santarini. Boat excursions operate from May to October. Popular trips include cruises to the offshore islands of Spinalonga, Yaidouronisi (Chrysi) and Dia.

From Hania there are day excursions to the Dikt ynna Temple, and from several resorts there are boat trips to unspoilt and otherwise inaccessible beaches. Ferries link the south coast resorts of Palaiochora, Souyia, Agia Roumeli, Loutro and Chora Sfakíon. From Soúyia, Palaióhora and Hóra Sfakíon ferries operate to the island of Gavdos south of Crete.

**Urban transport**  Iráklio is the only major conurbation on Crete but because of the one-way system and the central location of the sites and shops, most tourists tend to walk. The city has three bus stations, operating services to different regions of Crete. Buses for Knossos leave from a stop adjacent to the east-bound bus station.

## TAXIS

Taxis on Crete are plentiful and can be hailed in the street or picked up at taxi ranks. Check the meter is switched on or, if there is no meter, agree a price in advance. There are some fixed price journeys within towns and from the airports.

## FARES AND TICKETS

Travelling in Crete is much cheaper than in most European countries. Even taxis offer a viable way of getting round, and many local people use them for when the bus timetables are not convenient. Bus fares are very reasonable. In bigger towns where there is a proper bus station you can get your ticket and book a seat in advance, but the general rule is 'first come, first served'. A few concessions are available, mainly for students and schoolchildren.

## DRIVING

- The Greek drive on the right side of the road.
- Speed limit on national highway: 100kph (62mph) for cars.
- Speed limit on country roads: 80kph (49mph).
- Speed limit in built up areas: 50kph (31mph).
- Seat belts must be worn in both front and rear seats. Children under 10 must sit in the rear.
- Drink-driving is heavily penalized. Tolerance is a blood alcohol level of 0.05 per cent of alcohol.
- Petrol is readily available in the towns, but it's wise to fill up if you are touring. Super (95 octane), unleaded, super unleaded and diesel are available. Service stations are open Mon–Fri, 7am–7pm, Sat 7am–3pm. Some stay open until midnight and open Sun 7am–7pm.
- Members of motoring organizations are entitled to free breakdown service from the Greek motoring organization, ELPA, ☎ 104 in emergencies. Non-members should dial 174 for assistance. Car hire companies should also be notified as they often have own procedures.

## CAR RENTAL

Crete has numerous car rental firms, including all the internationally known names. Check if the price includes tax, collision damage waivers and unlimited mileage.

# Being there

## TOURIST OFFICES

- Odós Xanthoudídou,
  1 Platía Eleftherías (opposite
  Archaeological Museum)
  Iráklio
  ☎ (2810) 228225 or 228203

- Iráklio Airport; Iráklio
  ☎ (2810) 244462

- Odós Aktí I. Koundoúrou, 20
  (between the lake and the
  harbour)
  Agios Nikolaos, Lasithiou
  ☎ (28410) 22357

- Prıkıméa Eleıthérios Venizélos (on
  seafront east of the harbour)
  Rethymno
  ☎ (28310) 29148

- Inside the town hall
  Odós Khydonías 29, Hania
  ☎ (28210) 92000;
  www.chania.gr

- Venizélos Street
  Paleóhora, Hania
  ☎ (28230) 41507

- Waterfront, near Plateía
  Polytechniou Sitía,
  Lasithiou
  ☎ (28430) 28300

- Palaikastro
  Sitía 72300, Lasithiou
  ☎ (28430) 61546;
  www.palaikastro.com

## MONEY

The euro (€) is the official currency of Greece. Banknotes are issued in denominations of 5, 10, 20, 50, 100, 200 and 500 euros; coins in denominations of 1, 2, 5, 10, 20 and 50 cents, and 1 and 2 euros.

## TIPS/GRATUITIES

| Yes ✓   No ✗ | | |
| --- | --- | --- |
| Hotels (if service not inc.) | ✓ | 10% |
| Restaurants (if service not inc.) | ✓ | 10% |
| Cafés/Bars (if service not inc.) | ✓ | 10% |
| Taxis | ✓ | Change |
| Porters | ✓ | €1 a bag |
| Tour Guides | ✓ | Discretionary |
| Toilets | ✓ | Discretionary |

## POSTAL SERVICES

Post offices in the towns and larger villages are identified by yellow signs. In summer mobile offices operate in tourist areas. Post offices usually open 7:30–2:30 Monday to Friday, but in Iráklio and Hania they're open until 7:30. Some mobile post offices also open at weekends. Stamps can be bought at shops or kiosks selling postcards.

## TELEPHONES

Public telephones take a phone card, available locally in units of 100, 200, 500 and 1000. Some kiosks, shops and cafés have telephones with meters that can be used for international calls. OTE (Greek Telecom) have telephone exchanges in the larger resorts where you can make calls from booths and pay in cash afterwards.

### International dialling codes

From Crete dial:
UK 00 44
Germany 00 49
USA & Canada 00 1
Netherlands 00 31
Spain 00 34

### Emergency telephone numbers

General emergency/Police 100
Ambulance 166
Fire 199
Road assistance 104 (EPLA) or 174

## EMBASSIES AND CONSULATES

**UK** ☎ (2810) 224012 (Iráklio)
**France** ☎ (2810) 285618 (Iráklio)
**Germany**
☎ (2810) 226288 (Iráklio)
☎ (28210) 68876 (Hania)

**Netherlands**
☎ (2810) 343299 (Iráklio)
**USA** (Athens Embassy)
☎ (210) 721 2951

## HEALTH ADVICE

**Sun advice** Crete enjoys sunshine for most of the year, and from April/May until September it is almost constant. During July and August, when the sun is at its hottest, a hat, strong-protection sunscreen and plenty of non-alcoholic fluids are recommended.
**Drugs** Pharmacies have a large green or red cross outside the shop and sell most internationally known drugs and medicines over the counter or by prescription. Most pharmacies have someone who can speak English.

Opening hours are the same as those of shops, with a rota system at weekends.

**Safe water** Tap water is quite safe but because of the high level of minerals it does not suit all tourists. Bottled water is available everywhere at a reasonable cost.

## PERSONAL SAFETY

The crime rate in Crete is very low. Visitors can stroll through the streets without any threat, though unescorted women should not be surprised if they attract the Mediterranean roving eye. Whilst petty crime is minimal, it's wise to take simple precautions:

- Safeguard against attracting the attention of pickpockets.
- Leave valuables and important documents in the hotel or apartment safe.
- Lock car doors and never leave valuables visible inside.
- Police assistance: ☎ 100 from any call box

## ELECTRICITY

The power supply is 220 volts AC, 50hz; with sockets taking taking continental 2 round-pinned plugs. Visitors from the UK should bring an adaptor. Visitors from the USA will need a transformer for appliances using different voltages.

## OPENING HOURS

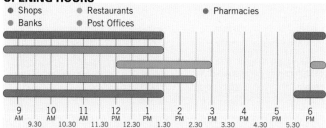

- Shops
- Banks
- Restaurants
- Post Offices
- Pharmacies

9 AM / 9.30 / 10 AM / 10.30 / 11 AM / 11.30 / 12 PM / 12.30 / 1 PM / 1.30 / 2 PM / 2.30 / 3 PM / 3.30 / 4 PM / 4.30 / 5 PM / 5.30 / 6 PM

In addition to the times shown above, many shops in tourist areas stay open daily from 8am to late evening. Banks close at the weekend and on public holidays. Opening hours of museums and archaeological sites vary enormously with many being closed on Mondays.

## LANGUAGE

The official language of Crete is Greek. Many of the locals speak English, but a few words of Greek can be useful in rural areas where locals may know no English. It is also useful to know the Greek alphabet – particularly for reading street names and road signs. A few useful words and phrases are listed below, with phonetic transliterations and accents to show emphasis.

| | | | |
|---|---|---|---|
| yes | *né* | I don't understand | *katalavéno* |
| no | *óhi* | | *...adío or yásas,* |
| please | *parakaló* | goodbye | *yásoo* |
| thank you | *efharistó* | sorry | *signómi* |
| hello | *yásas, yásoo* | how much? | *póso káni?* |
| good morning | *kalí méra* | where is...? | *poú eené..?* |
| good evening | *kalí spéra* | help! | *voíthia!* |
| good night | *kalí níkhta* | my name is... | *meh léne* |
| excuse me | *me sinchoríte* | I don't speak Greek | *then miló helliniká* |

| | | | |
|---|---|---|---|
| hotel | *xenodhohío* | toilet | *twaléta* |
| room | *dhomátyo* | bath | *bányo* |
| ...single/double | *monó/dhipló* | shower | *doos* |
| for three people | *ya tría átoma* | hot water | *zestó neró* |
| breakfast | *proinó* | key | *klidhí* |
| guest house | *pansyón* | towel | *petséta* |

| | | | |
|---|---|---|---|
| bank | *trápeza* | exchange rate | *isotimía* |
| exchange office | *ghrafío* | credit card | *pistotikí kárta* |
| | *sinalághmatos* | traveller's cheque | *taxidhyotikí epitayí* |
| post office | *tahidhromío* | passport | *dhiavatíryn* |
| money | *leftá* | cheap | *ftinós* |
| how much? | *póso káni?* | expensive | *akrivós* |

| | | | |
|---|---|---|---|
| restaurant | *estiatório* | dessert | *epidhórpyo* |
| café | *kafenío* | waiter | *garsóni* |
| menu | *menóo* | the bill | *loghariazmós* |
| lunch | *yévma* | bread | *psomi* |
| dinner | *dhípno* | water | *nero* |

| | | | |
|---|---|---|---|
| wine | *krasi* | coffee | *kafés* |
| coffee | *kafés* | waitress | *servitóra* |
| fruit | *fróoto* | tea (black) | *tsái* |

| | | | |
|---|---|---|---|
| aeroplane | *aeropláno* | ...port/harbour | *limáni* |
| airport | *aerodhrómio* | | *isitírio* |
| bus | *leoforío* | ticket | *apló/metepistrofís* |
| ...station | *stathmós* | car | *aftokínito* |
| ...stop | *stási* | taxi | *taxí* |
| boat | *karávi* | timetable | *dhromolóyo* |
| | | petrol | *venzíni* |

## GREEK ALPHABET

The Greek alphabet cannot be transliterated into other languages in a straightforward way. This can lead to variations in romanized spellings of Greek words and place-names. It also leads inevitably to inconsistencies, especially when comparing different guide books, leaflets and signs. However, the differences rarely make any name unrecognizable. The language looks complex, but it is worth memorizing the alphabet to help with signs, destinations etc.

| | | | | | |
|---|---|---|---|---|---|
| Alpha | Αα | *short a, as in hat* | Pi | Ππ | *p sound* |
| Beta | Ββ | *v sound* | Rho | Ρρ | *r sound* |
| Gamma | Γγ | *guttural g sound* | Sigma | Σσ | *s sound* |
| Delta | Δδ | *hard th, as in father* | Tau | Ττ | *t sound* |
| Epsilon | Εε | *short e* | Upsilon | Υυ | *ee, or y as in funny* |
| Zita | Ζζ | *z sound* | Phi | Φφ | *f sound* |
| Eta | Ηη | *long e, as in feet* | Chi | Χχ | *guttural ch, as in loch* |
| Theta | Θθ | *soft th, as in think* | Psi | Ψψ | *ps, as in chops* |
| Iota | Ιι | *short i, as in hit* | Omega | Ωω | *long o, as in bone* |
| Kappa | Κκ | *k sound* | | | |
| Lambda | Λλ | *l sound* | | | |
| Mu | Μμ | *m sound* | | | |
| Nu | Νν | *n sound* | | | |
| Xi | Ξξ | *x or ks sound* | | | |
| Omicron | Οο | *short o, as in pot* | | | |

# Best places to see

# 1 Agia Triada (Minoan Summer Palace)

**Linked to Phaestos by paved road, the dramatically sited Agia Triada is believed to have been the summer palace of Minoan royalty.**

Close to the more famous Minoan palace of Phaestos (▶ 40–41), Agia Triada enjoys an equally if not more spectacular setting, on a slope overlooking the Bay of Mésaras. Far fewer tourists

come here, and it is a delightful spot to explore. There is no record of the Minoan name ('Agia Triada' is the name of a nearby Byzantine chapel) and the purpose of another palace so close to Phaestos remains a mystery. The setting, which in Minoan times would have been far closer to the sea, and the elaborate decoration of the apartments, suggest this was a luxurious summer villa, possibly for use by the royalty of Phaestos. The original 'palace' was razed to the ground in the disaster of 1450BC and was not rebuilt until some 200 years later.

The best starting point is the Byzantine chapel. From here you can look down on the complex: to the left the grandest, sea-view apartments, which had flagstoned floors, gypsum and alabaster-faced walls, and in the corner room, fine frescoes. To the right is a group of storerooms with *pithoi* (large storage jars) and further to the right the main reception rooms. On the far side of the palace lie the ruins of a town with a porticoed row of shops.

Some of the most exquisite Minoan works of art in Iráklio's Archaeological Museum (➤ 24–25) were found here. These include three carved black stone vases (the Harvester Vase, Boxer Vase and the Chieftain Cup) and a painted sarcophagus.

✚ 136 E2 ✉ 3km (2 miles) west of Phaestos ☎ (28920) 91360 🕐 Nov, Sep–Jun daily (except Mon) 8:30–3; Jul–Oct, Aug daily 8–7:30 🖐 Moderate 🍴 Café (€) at Phaestos 🚌 Buses only as far as Phaestos (3km/2 miles)

# 2 Archaiologiko Mouseio, Iráklio

**The museum contains the world's richest collection of Minoan art, providing a vivid insight into the life of a highly cultured society.**

The rich collection of archaeological finds spans ten centuries, from early neolithic to Roman times; but the main emphasis is on the Minoan era, with treasures from Knossos, Phaestos and other ancient palaces of Crete.

The exhibits range from votive figurines, seal stones, cult vessels and gold jewellery to spearheads and sarcophagi. Outstanding are the exquisite pottery vessels of the Early and New Palace periods, and the tiny figures of animals and people, who are portrayed with an extraordinary degree of naturalistic detail. Among the individual highlights are the Phaestos Disc (➤ 41), the tiny faience figures of the bare-breasted Snake Goddesses, the bull's head *rhyton,* or ceremonial vessel and the tiny ivory acrobat in mid-air; and the three carved *rhytons* from Agia Triada (➤ 22–23): the Chieftain Cup, the Harvester Vase and the Boxer Vase.

The magnificent Minoan frescoes, mostly from the Palace of Knossos, are the highlight of the museum; for although they are heavily restored the lively, vividly coloured works of

art go to the heart of Minoan life. Dating from 1600–1400BC the frescoes are joyful, elegant depictions of man in harmony with nature, of ceremonies and worship and scenes of daily life.

Those who have visited Knossos may recognize many of the frescoes from the reproductions there, including *The Cup-Bearer* from the Procession fresco, the *Dolphins* from the Queen's apartments, the *Prince of the Lilies* and the famous *Bull-Leapers*. One of the oldest frescoes shows a female figure with an elaborate coiffure, sacral knot at the neck, large black eyes and red lips.

✚ 141 C7 ✉ Plateía Elefthérias (entrance on Odós Xanthoudídou), Iráklio ☎ (2810) 226092 ③ Closed for renovation at time of writing. Phone to check if it has reopened 👖 Expensive; free on Sun in winter 🍴 Cafeteria (€) beside the museum 🚌 Bus stop by the museum
ℹ Opposite the museum

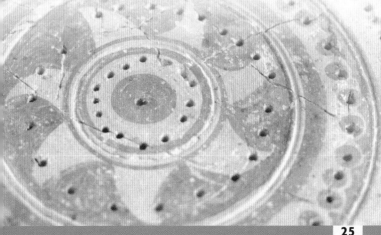

# 3 Farangi Samarias (Samaria Gorge)

**Towering peaks, plunging depths and springs of clear water – a dramatic setting for a walk through one of Europe's longest and deepest canyons.**

In high season up to 2,000 tourists a day walk the 16km (10 mile) gorge. The flood of walkers, mostly on guided tours, kills any real sense of adventure but the stunning mountain scenery is well worth the 5–7 hour hike. The gorge was designated a national park in 1962 in an attempt to preserve its wealth of flora and fauna. Most importantly the park was created to protect the famous Cretan wild goats, shy, nimble-footed animals that are unlikely to show themselves in the gorge.

The starting point at the head of the gorge is on the mountain-ringed Omalós plain, and by far the best plan is to arrive by public transport, hike through the gorge to Agia Rouméli and take a ferry from here to Hóra Sfakíon, then a bus back to Hania, the nearest main resort. The walk can be

quite demanding, particularly in the midsummer sun, and there are mules and a helicopter on hand to help those in trouble. Sturdy shoes are essential for negotiating the scree and crossing the river. Those daunted by the prospect of a 16km hike but eager to see the gorge have two options: either to do the first part of the walk, taking the breathtaking descent down the *xilóskala* ('wooden stairs'), with the disadvantage of the stiff climb back; or to start from Agia Rouméli, climbing 2km (1.6 miles) to the entrance, then continuing uphill into the gorge.

➕ 133 E5 ✉ 43km (27 miles) south of Hania ☎ (2810) 92287 or (2810) 67140 🕔 May–Oct, depending on weather, 6am–sunset ✋ Expensive 🍴 Tavernas (€€) at head of gorge and at Agia Rouméli; take refreshments for the gorge 🚌 From Hania to the head of the gorge on the Omalós Plain. From Hóra Sfakíon back to Hania; check times locally 🚢 In summer 4–5 ferries a day from Agia Rouméli to Hóra Sfakíon; daily afternoon ferry to Sougia and Paleochora
❓ For details of walk, ➤ 116–117
🛈 Head of the gorge

# 4 Gortys

**The ancient ruins, scattered among fields and hillsides, are eloquent evidence of the power of the former capital of Crete.**

Not so ancient as the famous Minoan sites – in fact, rather insignificant in those days – Gortys came to prominence under the Dorians, ousted Phaestos from its pinnacle by the 3rd century BC and attained the ultimate status of capital of Crete after the Roman invasion of 67BC. Its tentacles of power reached as far away as North Africa, but in AD824 the great city was destroyed by the Turks, and it has lain abandoned ever since.

Though the walls have crumbled and the columns have fallen, the extensive remains are a compelling evocation of the great city. The finely preserved apse of the 6th-century Basilica of Agios

Titos is built on the supposed site of martyrdom of St Titus, who was sent by St Paul to convert the islanders to Christianity. Nearby is the semi-circular Odeon, roofless now, but once a covered theatre where the Romans enjoyed musical concerts.

Behind the Odeon, protected now by a modern brick arcade, are perhaps the most precious remains of the site – the huge stone blocks engraved with the famous law code of Gortys which, dating from 500BC, represents the first known code of law in Europe. In its archaic Dorian dialect, written from right to left on one line, then from left to right on the next, the code deals with civil issues such as divorce, adultery, inheritance and property rights, giving a fascinating insight into Dorian life on Crete.

The remnants of the acropolis lie on a hill to the west, and there are more remains along the road towards Agia Déka (but no parking there).

✚ 136 E4 ✉ Agia Déka, Iráklio (46km/28.5 miles south of Iráklio, 8km/5 miles east of Moíres) ☎ (28920) 31144
🕐 May–Oct 8–7; Nov–Apr 8–6 ✋ Moderate
🍴 Café/bar (€) 🚌 Regular service from Iráklio

# 5 Hania Limani

**One of the most beautiful places on Crete is the Venetian harbour in Hania (also known as Chania).**

At night, when the sun goes down and the lights come on in the cafés and restaurants, the harbour truly comes into its element and is enchantingly pretty. Locals come out for their evening stroll up and down, there are children playing and everyone mixing with the crowds of visitors also enjoying their night out.

The Venetians arrived in the early 13th century, and bought the island of Crete for 100 silver marks from Boniface of Montferrat, who had received the island as part of his share of the spoils after taking part in the Fourth Crusade. The Venetians remained for about 400 years, till the island fell to the Turks. In their time here they built many fortresses, with their most attractive legacy being this harbour in

Hania and some of the lovely old mansions in the Old Towns of both Hania and Rethymno. Several of these have been turned into stylish hotels, and here in Hania some of them have rooftops looking out over the harbour, as they have done for a few hundred years.

Walk west around the harbour and you will come to the remains of the Venetian arsenals, where the builders and repairers of the Venetian ships were based. On your way you pass the Mosque of the Janissaries, which was built in 1645, the same year that the Turks captured the town and put an end to Venetian rule here. It is therefore the oldest Turkish building on Crete, and a reminder of the dramas that this harbour has seen, as a backdrop to the relaxed and peaceful atmosphere of today.

✚ 142 D2

# 6 Knossos

**The Minoan civilization grew and prospered around Knossos, the largest and most powerful of the palaces in Crete.**

A hundred years ago King Minos and Knossos were merely names from the myths of ancient Greece, but in 1894 British archaeologist Arthur Evans purchased a site that transpired to be the largest and most important palace in Crete and gave credence to the myths. Excavations, which began in 1900, revealed a complex of buildings, surrounded by a town of around 12,000 inhabitants. The elaborate rooms and the wealth of treasures discovered were evidence of a highly developed ancient civilization, but it was the labyrinth layout and the sacred symbols on walls and pillars that suggested Knossos as the seat of the legendary King Minos and home of the Minotaur. Hence Evans gave the name 'Minoan' to the newly discovered culture.

### Site Tour

Raised walkways have been erected around most of the site. Visitors enter by the west court, then follow the walkway to the Corridor of the Procession, with a copy of the original fresco of a procession of more than 500 figures. Steps lead up to the *piano nobile,* completely reconstructed and displaying reproductions of the palace's most famous frescoes. From here there are good views over the storerooms and *pithoi* (large storage jars). The terrace steps lead down to the Central Court, formerly used for religious rituals and bull-leaping displays. In the northwest corner the throne room contains the original 'Throne of Minos' and a lustral basin (sunken bath) for purification. The seat in the antechamber is a reproduction of Minos' throne. On the far side of the central court the grand staircase (closed for restoration) leads down to what Evans believed to be the royal apartments: The Hall of the Double Axes, the King's Megaron and the most elaborately decorated of all the rooms, the Queen's Megaron. This was decorated with the well-known leaping dolphin fresco, and equipped with a bathroom and a lavatory with drains. The walkway continues round to the north entrance with its reproduction of the Charging Bull fresco, and the theatre and Royal Road, said to be the oldest paved road in Europe.

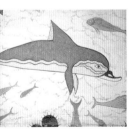

➕ 137 B5 ✉ 5km (3 miles) south of Iráklio ☎ (2810) 231940 ⊗ Daily 8–7:30 (5pm in winter) ✋ Expensive ❚❚ Café on site (€€), tavernas nearby 🚌 No 2 from Iráklio (Bus Station A) every 10 minutes ❓ Guided tours available in four languages. Shop with books and reproductions

# Moni Arkaiou

**The mass suicide within Moni Arkaiou came to symbolize Cretan heroism and strengthened the Cretan struggle against the Turkish yoke.**

The fame of Moni Arkaiou lies not so much in its splendid setting on a plateau in the Ída Mountains, nor in its beautiful baroque façade, but in the historic role it played during the struggle for freedom from Turkish rule in the 19th century. Isolated in the mountains, the monastery became an important centre of Cretan resistance, supporting uprisings against foreign powers.

On 9 November 1866, following a two-day siege, thousands of Turkish troops forced entry through the western gateway. Within the monastery hundreds of resistance fighters were taking refuge with their wives and children. Rather than suffer death at the hands of the Turks, the Cretans blew themselves up, so the story is told, by setting light to the powder magazine. Most of the Cretans within the monastery were killed, but so were hundreds of Turks – the exact number of deaths is unknown. Following the event many prominent figures in Europe rallied to support the Cretan cause, among them Garibaldi and Victor Hugo. Nearly a century later the writer Nikos Kazantzákis retold the historic event in his powerful novel, *Freedom and Death*.

Visitors to the monastery can see the richly carved Venetian façade, dating from 1587, the restored interior of the church, the roofless

powder magazine bearing scars of the explosion, and a small museum of icons, vessels and siege memorabilia. Close to the entrance to the monastery an ossuary containing the skulls of the siege victims is a chilling reminder of the events of 1866.

✚ 134 D4 ✉ 24km (15 miles) southeast of Rethymno ☎ (28310) 83116 🕐 Daily 8–7 💷 Moderate 🍽 Snack bar (€) on the premises, taverna (€) at Amnátos (4km/2.5 miles north) 🚌 Four buses a day from Rethymno

# 8 Moni Preveli

**www.**preveli.org

**The peaceful setting overlooking the southern sea and the monastery's historic past combine to make Preveli one of Crete's most compelling sights.**

When Crete fell to the Turks in the 17th century, the monks of Preveli decided to abandon their original monastery in favour of a more secluded location. Their new monastery, perched above the Libyan Sea, soon became a centre of resistance and grew wealthy on the olive groves, sheep, goats, wine, corn and other gifts that were bequeathed by

Cretans to prevent their possessions falling into Turkish hands.

More recently the monastery sheltered Allied troops after the fall of Crete to the Germans in 1941, and assisted their evacuation from nearby beaches to the Egyptian port of Alexandria.

Largely rebuilt in 1835, then partially destroyed by the Germans in reprisal for the protection of the soldiers, the monastery retains none of its original buildings, but it is still a handsome complex with splendid views.

The finest feature is the Church of Agios Ioánnis (St John), a 19th-century reconstruction of the original 17th-century church, containing an elaborate inconostasis with many old icons and a gold cross with diamonds, containing what is said to be a fragment of the True Cross. The story goes that the Germans tried three times to steal the cross but each time they tried to start their escape aircraft, the engines failed. A small museum within the church houses vestments, silverware, icons and votive offerings.

The church and remains of the early monastery, Káto Moni Preveli, can still be seen beside the Megapótomos River, 3km (2 miles) inland.

➕ 134 F2 ✉ 13km (8 miles) east of Plakias ☎ (28320) 31246 🕐 Summer daily 9–7; winter daily 9–5. Museum closes 1–3 ✋ Moderate 🍴 Snack bar (€) on premises in summer 🚌 Limited bus service from Rethymno

# Panagia Kera

**The beautifully restored Byzantine frescoes adorning the walls and domes of this tiny church are remarkable for their realism and drama.**

Set amid the olive and cypress trees of the Kritsa plain, this delightful little church dates back to the 13th and 14th centuries, and is a treasure house of religious art. Triangular buttresses supporting the aisles give the church an unusual appearance, but it is the interior, with the most complete series of Byzantine frescoes in Crete, that draws the crowds (arrive as early as possible to avoid the crush).

The only light in the church comes through the narrow apsidal windows and it takes time to

decipher the different scenes. The very oldest frescoes are those of the apse, followed by the scenes from the Life of Christ in the dome and nave. More easily recognizable are the nave scenes of *The Nativity*, *Herod's Banquet* and *The Last Supper*.

The later wall paintings of the south and north aisles show a marked move towards naturalism. In the south aisle (where you enter) the scenes from the life of St Anne and of the Virgin Mary are lively 14th-century frescoes, the faces full of expression. Note the face of Anne, whose portrait dominates the apse, and the touching scene in the aisle of Mary looking dejected over Joseph's misunderstood reaction to her conception. An angel descends to explain to Joseph. The north aisle frescoes portray scenes of the *Last Judgement*, depictions of St Anthony and other saints, and a portrait of the founder of the church with his wife and daughter.

✚ 138 D3 ✉ Kritsa, 10km (6 miles) southwest of Agios Nikolaos ☎ (28410) 51711 🕐 Mon–Sat 8–5, Sun 8–2 ✋ Moderate 🍴 Cafés on premises (€), Paradise Restaurant across the road (€€) 🚌 Regular service from Agios Nikolaos ❓ Icons and guides for sale at shop

# 10 Phaestos

**Second only to Knossos in importance, Phaestos dominated the Mesará Plain and was ruled by the legendary Rhadamanthys, brother of King Mínos.**

The most striking feature of Phaestos is its dramatic setting, on a ridge overlooking the rich Mesará Plain. Excavations by an Italian archaeologist in the early 20th century revealed that the development of Phaestos followed that of Knossos: the original palace was built around 1900BC, destroyed in 1700BC and replaced by a grander palace. Unlike Knossos, however, this second palace (destroyed in 1450BC) incorporated foundations from the first palace. This makes interpretation of the site somewhat confusing and time-consuming and there are no reconstructions (as at Knossos) to help, but the leaflet which comes with the admission ticket is quite useful.

Steps down from the entrance lead to the west court and theatre area via the upper court. The storage structures visible to the south of the

west court were probably used for grain. The grand staircase leads up to the New Palace, with rooms overlooking the Old Palace (fenced off and still undergoing excavation). The huge paved central court, which has fine views of the Psoloreítis range of mountains, was originally bordered by a portico, foundations of which can still be seen. To the north the royal apartments (closed) were the most elaborate of the rooms, with the best views. It was in one of the chambers beyond these apartments, at the northern edge of the site, that the excavators discovered the famous Phaestos Disc, now in Iráklio's Archaeological Museum (➤ 24–25). Small, round and made of clay, the disc is inscribed with spiralling hieroglyphics that defy translation.

✚ 136 E3 ✉ Phaestos, Iráklio (66km/41 miles southwest of Iráklio, 8km/5 miles west of Moíres) ☎ (28920) 91315 ⊙ May–Oct daily 8–7:30; Nov–Mar daily 8–5 ✋ Moderate ¶ Cafeteria (€) on the premises 🚌 Regular service from Iráklio ℹ Tourist Pavilion on the premises

# Exploring

Crete is the one Greek island that has something for everyone. In part that is because it is the largest Greek island, but it's also because it has always been a proud and independent island, holding onto its traditions.

For most visitors, Crete's superb beaches, especially along the busy north coast with its large resorts, are reason enough to visit. Those interested in history and culture will find satisfaction in the numerous archaeological remains, of which the best-known is the world-famous Knossos, a UNESCO World Heritage Site.

Nature lovers and hikers will discover that Crete is a wonderful island, filled with challenges and secrets as well as more famous places like the Samaria Gorge. Walking or riding is enhanced by the prospect of seeing eagles, vultures or the rare lammergeier, and orchids, irises, poppies or some of Crete's other 1,500 plant species. Crete is indeed a Greek island like no other.

# Iráklio Province

**In the centre of the island, Iráklio is the most visited of all the provinces. Not only does it embrace the four great Minoan sites at Knossos, Phaestos, Malia and Agia Triada, but in Limin Hersónisou and Malia it also has the two biggest resorts on Crete.**

Iráklio itself is a bustling, traffic-ridden city but this should not deter sightseers from a visit to the Archaeological Museum, which houses the world's greatest collection of Minoan artefacts. Few tourists actually stay in the city, most preferring the beach resorts to the east. While the north coast has a long ribbon of tourist development, the south coast is far less accessible, with just a handful of small resorts. Of these, the one-time hippie haunt of Matala, with a fine beach and rock caves, is the most developed.

## IRÁKLIO TOWN

Fifth largest city in Greece, Iráklio is the capital of
Crete and the commercial and cultural hub of the
island. Herakleium to the Romans, Rabdh-el-Khandak
(Castle of the Ditch) to the Saracens, Candia to the
Venetians, Megélo Kástro (Great Fortress) to the
Turks, it finally reverted to Herákleion (or Iráklio) in
1923. Badly damaged by bombs during World War II,
it is today an essentially modern city.

Once a dusty town with an eastern flavour, Iráklio
is now taking on a cosmopolitan air. Fashionable
young people fill the cafés and smart boutiques sell
the latest designs.

Everything of cultural interest lies conveniently
within the ramparts and can easily be covered on

foot. The most
colourful quarter is
the harbour, where
fishermen gut their
catch and skinny
cats sniff around for
titbits. The fortress
overlooking the
harbour and the
nearby vaults of the
arsenals are prominent reminders of the city's
Venetian heyday. In the central Plateía Venizélos,
cafés cluster around the fountain. From here the
pedestrianized Odós Daidálos, lined with shops
and tavernas, leads on to the huge Plateía Elefthérias
and the famous Archaeological Museum (▶ 24–25).

Most of the architecture is postwar, but there are a
number of old ruins or fountains and some neo-
classical buidings. The Venetian walls, 40m (131ft)

thick in places, were constructed in 1462 on earlier Byzantine foundations, and extended in 1538. Most of the gates survive, and it is possible to walk along the line of the walls for about 4km (2.5 miles), though only 1km (0.6 miles) of the walk is actually on top of the walls. Near here, is the tomb of Nikos Kazantzákis – Crete's most famous writer.
✚ 137 B5

### Agia Ekaterini (Museum of Religious Art)

Within the Church of Agia Ekaterini (St Catherine), the Museum of Religious Art houses the most important collection of icons in Crete. During the 16th and 17th centuries the church was part of the Mount Sinai Monastery School, which became one of the centres of the 'Cretan Renaissance'. The style of painting was characterized by the intermingling of Byzantine iconography with elements inspired by the Western Renaissance. One of the pupils here was Mikhaíl Damaskinós, and the six icons by him, on the right as you go in, are the finest works of art in the museum. Doménico Theotokópoulos, commonly known as El Greco, may have been one of his contemporaries.

✚ 141 C5 ✉ Plateía Aikaterinis ☎ (2810) 288825 🕐 Mon–Sat 9–1, Tue, Thu, Fri also 5–7; Jan and Dec, mornings only 💰 Moderate 🍴 Cafés (€) in Plateía Aikaterinis

### Archaiologiko Mouseio
Best places to see ➤ 24–25.

### Agios Markos

The Basilica of St Mark, fronted by an arcaded portico, was built in 1239 by the Venetians and dedicated to their patron saint. The first church was destroyed by an earthquake in 1303 and its successor followed the same fate in 1500, but it was rebuilt and, like many others on Crete, became a mosque under the Turks. It later fell into decline but was restored in 1956–61 and today serves as an exhibition hall. Look out for the marble doorway inside, which is decorated with bunches of grapes.

✚ 141 C6 ✉ Odós 25 Avgoústou ☎ (2810) 399228 ◷ Daily 9–1 and some evenings ✋ Free

### Agios Petrou Dominikanon

Just to the northeast of the Historical Museum of Crete, the evocative ruins and arches of Agios Petrou lie between the sea and graffiti-splattered modern buildings. The church was built by Dominican monks in the first half of the 13th century and converted into the mosque of Sultan Ibrahim under the Turks. The southern chapel preserves the only 15th-century frescoes in Iráklio, but the church is currently undergoing restoration and is temporarily closed to the public.

✚ 141 A5 ✉ Odós Sofoklí Venizélou ☎ None

### Agios Titos

Named after the saint who was sent by St Paul to convert the Cretans to Christianity, this building has had a chequered history. The Byzantine church was rebuilt several times after earthquakes, converted into a mosque by the Turks, ruined by another earthquake in 1856, rebuilt again, and, in 1923, reconsecrated to St Titus. The chapel to the left, by the entrance, houses a gold reliquary chalice containing the head of St Titus. This precious relic was taken to Venice for safekeeping when Iráklio fell to the Turks; it was finally returned to its rightful home in 1966 – 300 years later.

✚ 141 B6 ✉ Odós 25 Avgoústou ☎ (2810) 346221 ⏰ Mon–Sat 8–12, 5–7 ✋ Free 🍴 Cafés and restaurants (€–€€) on Plateía Ágiou Titou

### Istoriko Mouseio Kritis

The Historical Museum of Crete takes up the story where the Archaeological Museum (➤ 24–25) leaves off and provides a fascinating insight into the island's turbulent history, from the early Christian era to the 20th century. Slightly away from the city centre, the museum is very pleasant to explore.

The collection starts with an exhibition of artefacts from the Christian period, with emphasis on the Venetian occupation and the Cretan War (1645–1669). This is illustrated by plans, photographs, clear explanations and a highly detailed model of Candia (Iráklio) in 1645. On the same floor the Ceramics Room illustrates the way in which pottery has evolved over 15 centuries.

The Medieval and Renaissance section displays Byzantine, Venetian and Turkish sculpture, Cretan-school icons, coins, jewellery and a collection of copies of Byzantine frescoes from Cretan churches. An early painting by El Greco depicts a stormy View of Mount Sinai (1570), with tiny figures of pilgrims climbing up the craggy peak to the Monastery of St Catherine.

The struggle for Cretan independence and the period of autonomy (1898–1908) is illustrated by portraits of revolutionaries, flags, weapons and photographs. The reconstructions of the studies of the writer Níkos Kazantzákis and Emmanuel Tsouderós, Greek Prime Minister at the time of the Battle of Crete, bring you into the 20th century. The folk rooms on the fourth floor display local crafts and

contain a replica of
a traditional village
home.
**www.**historical-
museum.gr

🚩 141 B5 ✉ Limáchou
Kalokairinoú 7 ☎ (2810)
283219 🕐 Apr–Oct
Mon–Sat 9–5; Nov–Mar
Mon–Sat 9–5 and also
Wed 6–9 💷 Moderate
🍴 Waterfront
restaurants nearby
(€–€€)

## Koules Fortress

Guarding the harbour, the mighty Koules fortress was built by the Venetians in the 16th century on the foundations of an earlier fort. Various strongholds had occupied the site since the Saracens arrived in the 9th century, but none as huge and impregnable as the Venetian structure. Called Rocca al Mare by the Venetians, it resisted the Turks for 21 years, finally surrendering in 1669. The winged lion of St Mark – symbol of Venice – decorates three sides of the fort, the best preserved on the far, seaward side.

There is little to see inside the fort, but the cool chambers and the walk along the causeway beyond the fortress provide welcome respite from the bustle of the town. From the top there are fine views of the harbour, town and the towering peaks of the Psoloreítis in the distance. Clearly visible across the street from the harbour are the vaulted chambers of the Arsenali, where the Venetian war galleys were built and repaired. The shipyards were built between the 13th and the 17th centuries.

✚ 141 A6 ✉ Iráklio Harbour ☎ (2810) 246211 ③ Jul–Oct daily 8–7:30; Nov–Jun daily 9–3 (but erratic) 🐾 Moderate ❓ Opening hours vary during temporary exhibitions. Upper storey used as an open-air theatre in summer

## Krini Morosini (Morozíni Fountain)

The central feature of Plateía Venizélos, the Morozíni fountain was built in 1628 by Francesco Morosini, Venetian Governor of the island. A 16km (10-mile) long aqueduct was built to channel water to it from Mount Gioúchtas in the south. The fountain, which is rarely in action, has eight circular basins, decorated with reliefs of nymphs, tritons, dolphins, mermaids, cherubs and mythical creatures. Above, the 14th-century carved lions were incorporated into the fountain and formerly supported a statue of Neptune. Plateía Venizélos (familiarly known as Fountain Square) is the tourist centre of Iráklio, and is packed with bustling cafés and restaurants.

✚ 141 C5 ✉ Plateía Venizélos

## More to see in Iráklio Province

### AGIA TRIADA
Best places to see ➤ 22–23.

### CRETAQUARIUM
This large, modern aquarium near Gournes is a wonderful new attraction on Crete, devoted to displaying the diversity of Mediterranean marine life. Huge tanks show the wide array of sea creatures that live off Crete's shores and further afield, while educating people, especially children, as to their importance. One display concentrates on creatures which live 'Far from Light', such as the spiny lobster, the conger eel, the dusky grouper, the scorpion fish and the European lobster. Another deals with the open sea, another with the life of the shore, and there is an impressive tank devoted solely to the much-feared jellyfish.

**www.**cretaquarium.gr
✚ 137 B6 ✉ 15km (9 miles) east of Iráklio ☎ (2810) 337788 🕐 Mon–Sat May to mid-Oct 9–9, mid-Oct to Apr 10–5:30 ✋ Moderate

### FODELE
Fodele is the birthplace of El Greco – or it claims to be. Scholars argue that the painter was born in Iráklio. In any event the village makes a pleasant detour, along a verdant valley of orange and lemon groves.

Over the bridge, streets are lined by rustic, flower-decked dwellings. The **El Greco House** is well signposted, and lies about 1km from the centre, opposite the Byzantine Church of the Panagía.

✚ 136 B4 ✉ 19km (12 miles) northwest of Iráklio, 3km (2 miles) south of the E75 🍴 Taverna El Greco (€) 🚌 2 per day from Iráklio

**Smiti El Greco (El Greco House)**

✉ Opposite the Byzantine Church of the Panagía
☎ (2810) 521500
🕐 May–Oct Tue–Sun 9–5
🖐 Inexpensive

## GORTYS

Best places to see ➤ 28–29.

## KNOSSOS

Best places to see ➤ 32–33.

## LIMIN HERSÓNISOU

Packed with holidaymakers in pursuit of fun and sun, Limin Hersónisou and neighbouring Malia make up the biggest tourist development on Crete. The strips of grey sand and pebble are barely sufficient to cope with the crowds, but many visitors opt to spend long hours in sea-view bars anyway. Nightlife centres on the discos, clubs and bars, some of which operate all night long.

A walk around the harbour provides a pleasant break from the bustle as well as fine views of the mountains towering behind the high-rise blocks. A seaport thrived here in ancient times but only vestiges survive of its ancient splendour. The submerged remains of the Roman harbour are just visible off the headland and, amid the video bars, souvenirs and boutiques on the seafront, you can see the fenced-in fragments of a fish mosaic which was originally part of a Roman fountain.

The resort offers a variety of nearby diversions. The Lychnostatis (Cretan Open-Air Museum) gives an insight into authentic Cretan life. At Piskopianó's **Museum of Rural Life** workshops and agricultural tools are displayed within an old olive-oil mill. To the east and south of the resort, explore the slides and rides of the Star Water Park and the Aqua Splash Water Park.

✚ 137 B7 ⊠ 28km (17 miles) east of Iráklio 🚌 Regular buses from Iráklio
🍴 Countless bars and tavernas in the centre (€–€€)

**Agrotileo Mouseio Limin Hersónisou (Museum of Rural Life)**
⊠ Piskopianó (3km/2 miles south of Limin Hersónisou) ☎ (28970) 23303
🕐 Apr–Oct daily 10–7

## MALIA

To the east of this resort lie the ancient Minoan remains of **Malia Palace.** The ruins are not as spectacular as those of Knossos, but the setting, on a quiet stretch of the coast between the sea and Lasithiou mountains, is rather more impressive. Those who have visited Knossos or Phaestos will recognize the layout around the central court, with store-rooms, ceremonial stairways, royal apartments and lustral basin. The origins are similar too. The palace was built in around 1900BC but destroyed by an earthquake in 1700BC. A second palace was built on the foundations, but (unlike Knossos) it was completely destroyed in the unknown catastrophe of 1450BC. Among the many treasures discovered here were an axe head in the shape of a leopard and a sword with a crystal hilt, both of which are now in the Archaeological Museum, Iráklio (➤ 24–25).

French archaeologists are continuing to excavate a town which lay to the north and west of the palace. A 10-minute walk northeast towards the sea brings you to the Khrysólakkos (Pit of Gold), a burial site where priceless jewellery was discovered,

including an exquisite gold bee pendant, also in the Iráklio Museum. The unashamedly brash and rowdy resort of Malia – along with neighbouring Limín Hersónisou (➤ 56) – is the party capital of the island. Packed with discos, video bars and burger joints, it is similar to Limín Hersónisou, but has a far better beach, with sands stretching a considerable distance to the east.

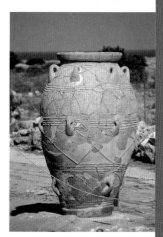

✚ 137 B8 ✉ 36km (22 miles) east of Iráklio ☗ Large choice in the centre (€–€€) ☐ Regular service from Iráklio

**Anakforo Malia (Malia Palace)**
✉ 3km (2 miles) east of Malia ☎ (28970) 31597 ⏰ Tue–Sun 8:30–7 ✋ Moderate; free on Sun in winter ☗ Café/bar on premises; restaurants (€–€€) in Malia (3km/2 miles) ☐ Regular service from Malia and Iráklio

## MATALA

Matala made its name in the 1960s when foreign hippies (Cat Stevens and Bob Dylan among them) took advantage of the free accommodation offered by the historic rock caves. Unpopular with both locals and archaeologists, the hippies were thrown out long ago. Today Matala attracts tourists of all ages, but it still appeals in particular to independent travellers. The climate is milder than the north coast and sunsets can be enjoyed from the beach tavernas and bars, one of which, Lion's Bar, calls itself the Last Bar Before Africa – true if it wasn't for the island of Gavdos (➤ 115). Matala's main attraction is its sand and shingle beach, sheltered between sloping ochre-coloured cliffs which are riddled with man-made caves. The caves range from small hacked-out holes to rooms with carved benches, steps, windows and fireplaces. No-one knows who made the original caves, but they are believed to have been Roman or early Christian tombs. The sands are very crowded in summer. Behind the beach the village now caters almost entirely for tourists, but the resort is still pleasantly free of high-rise buildings, as much of the accommodation is in guest houses. There are boat trips to smaller beaches further south or you can walk over the rocks (about 20 minutes) to Red Beach, named after its reddish-brown sands.

✚ 136 E2 ✉ 70km (43 miles) southwest of Iráklio ⏰ Caves 11:30–7 ✋ Caves free 🍴 Cafés and tavernas (€–€€) on the beach 🚌 Services from Iráklio, Moíres and Phaestos

## MOUSEIO FYSIKIS ISTORIAS KRITIS (NATURAL HISTORY MUSEUM)

Crete's wildlife, plants and landscape are attractively presented in this museum, set in a modern building outside the city walls on the road to Knossos. If you are planning a trip to the countryside or a drive around the island it will certainly enhance your appreciation of the things you will see. Life-sized dioramas on the ground floor recreate the island's flora and fauna in their natural habitats. Displays highlight birdlife and endangered species such as the Cretan wild goat, or *kri-kri*, which can still be seen in areas of Crete such as the Samaria Gorge. Glass cases in the gift shop house live snakes, the curious ocellated skink and the Cretan spiny mouse. The botanical garden is filled with aromatic wild herbs, while upstairs exhibits focus on the island's geological and human evolution.

**www**.nhmc.uoc.gr

✚ 137 B5 ✉ Odós Knosuou 157 ☎ (2810) 324711 🕙 Under renovation at time of writing 💷 Free 🍴 Coffee shop on site (€) 🚌 2, 3, 4 from Irakleío

## MYRTIA

Myrtia is a pretty place to visit, surrounded by vines and full of flowers and potted plants. It is proud of its Kazantzákis connection, and announces the museum at either end of the village in five languages. Níkos Kazantzákis' father lived on the central square in a large house which has been converted into a **museum** dedicated to the writer. Best known for his novel, *Zorba the Greek*, Kazantzákis was also a poet, travel journalist and essayist. The museum houses a collection of first editions of his books, costumes from his plays, stills from films of his books, photographs and personal belongings.

✚ 137 C6 ✉ 16km (10 miles) southeast of Irákli 🍴 Cafés (€) in the square

**Níkos Kazantzákis Museum**

☎ (2810) 742451 🕙 Fri–Wed 9–1, 4–8 💷 Moderate

## PHAESTÓS

Best places to see ➤ 40–41.

## TILISOS

Reached off the old Iráklio/Rethymno national road, and set in the mountains, surrounded by olive groves and vineyards, Tilisos is home to three Minoan villas dating from the New Palace period (1700–1450BC). Like Knossos and Phaestos, which were built at the same time, there are signs of earlier structures. Excavated in the 20th century, the villas are referred to as Houses A, B and C, the best preserved being A (straight ahead as you enter the site) and C (the house on the left).

The ruins are far less imposing than those of the famous Minoan palaces, but it is interesting to see where lesser mortals lived – it is also a delightful, peaceful spot for a stroll. House A, largest of the villas, has storerooms with reconstructed *pithoi* (large storage jars), a court with columns, a lustral basin and stairs which indicate an upper floor. House C is the most elaborate of the three.

✚ 136 B4 ✉ 10km (6 miles) west of Iráklio ☎ (2810) 226470
🕐 Tue–Sun 8:30–3 👋 Moderate 🍴 Taverna (€) next to the site
🚌 Service from Iráklio

## VORI

The old village of Vori was put on the tourist map in 1985 when it became the home of the excellent **Mouseio Kritikis Ethnologia (Museum of Cretan Ethnology).** In 1992 a further boost came with the award of Best European Museum by the Council of Europe. Inconspicuously located in a building near the church, it is a modern museum with exhibits beautifully laid out behind glass and informatively labelled. Devoted to traditional crafts and ways of life in rural Crete, the museum has

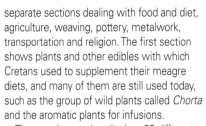

separate sections dealing with food and diet, agriculture, weaving, pottery, metalwork, transportation and religion. The first section shows plants and other edibles with which Cretans used to supplement their meagre diets, and many of them are still used today, such as the group of wild plants called *Chorta* and the aromatic plants for infusions.

The weaving section displays 25 different types of baskets made of reed, wild olive, rush, myrtle and other natural materials. The baskets served a variety of purposes, from trapping fish, harvesting sultana grapes and keeping snails to draining cheese. Pottery, made in Crete since Minoan times, includes vessels for *rakí*, vinegar and water, and storage pots for oil, wine, cereals and honey.

➕ 136 E2 ✉ 4km (2.5 miles) north of Phaestos
🍴 Tavernas (€–€€) 🚌 Service from Iráklio

**Mouseio Kritikis Ethnologia**

☎ (28920) 91112 🕐 Apr–Oct daily 10–6; in winter by appointment (☎ (28920) 91110) ✋ Moderate

# Lasithiou Province

**This eastern province may not boast the majestic mountains of central or western Crete, but it has plenty of other attractions, both scenic and cultural.**

The main tourist resort is Agios Nikolaos, overlooking the beautiful Gulf of Mirampéllou. From here the main road snakes its way to Sitia, hub of the eastern end of Crete and a base for the beaches of Vái and Ítanos. Further south lie the ancient remains of the palace of Zakros, one of the major Minoan sites on the island. The most dramatic geographical feature of the region is the Lasithiou Plateau, whose flat, fertile fields are ringed by the towering peaks of the Díkti Mountains. The south coast, where plastic greenhouses proliferate, is less scenic than the north, with little development. Ierapetra, the main town, has limited attractions for tourists.

### AGIOS NIKOLAOS

From a peaceful little harbour town, Agios Nikolaos (or 'Ag Nik' as English-speaking regulars like to call it) has grown into the most popular resort on Crete. In the Hellenistic era this was the port for Lato, whose archaeological remains can be seen in the hills to the west (▶ 79). The town fell into decline under the Romans but was later developed by the Venetians, who built a fort dominating the Bay of Mirampéllou (Beautiful View). In 1303 this was damaged by an earthquake, then later razed to the ground by the Turks. In 1870 Sfakiots from western Crete settled at the port, naming it after the Byzantine church of Agios Nikolaos to the north. The town today may not boast the architectural features and historic background of

Crete's other regional capitals; nonetheless it is a very picturesque resort with a lively atmosphere that appeals to all ages. There is nothing particularly Cretan about it, and the chief attraction is, and always has been, the setting on a hilly promontory overlooking the deep blue Gulf of Mirampéllou.

In the centre of the resort tavernas and cafés cluster around the busy fishing harbour and the deep-water Lake Voulisméni, which is linked to the harbour by a short canal. By day the main activity is strolling around the quaysides, browsing at souvenirs and whiling away the hours over lunch. Evening life centres on bars with music, cafés with cocktails and some discos. Luxury hotels provide pristine beaches, but public bathing areas leave much to be desired. The small strips of shingle and rock are invariably crowded, but you can walk or bus to the sandy beach of Almirós, 2km (1.2 miles) to the south.

A steep walk up from the port leads to the **Archaiologiko Mouseio (Archaeological Museum).** Dating from the 1970s this is a modern museum with a small collection of locally found treasures that were previously housed in the Archaeological Museum in Iráklio, and it is well worth a visit. Exhibits are arranged chronologically, from the early Minoan and neolithic period (6000–2100 BC) to the Graeco-Roman era. The emphasis is on Minoan works of art including terracotta figures of deities, Vasilikí flameware vases, seal stones, pottery and jewellery. The prize piece is the early Minoan Goddess of Mirtos in Room II – a stylized, libation vessel in the

form of a clay figure (c2500 BC) with a fat body, long skinny neck and tiny head, clasping a water jug. In the same room the beautiful gold jewellery in the form of ribbons, leaves and flowers, came from the island off Mohlos (► 80). The late Minoan 'larnakes' or clay sarcophagi in the next room were also used as bath tubs – one of them still contains the bones of two bodies. In Room IV, a rare late Minoan infant burial tomb is displayed as it was found. In the last room the grinning 1st century AD skull, bearing a wreath of gold olive leaves, was discovered at the Potamós necropolis near Agios Nikolaos. The silver coin found in its mouth is the fare for the ferry ride to the Underworld, across the mythical River Styx. The tiny **Mouseio Laographiko (Folk Museum)** near the tourist office is devoted mainly to folk art. Among the local crafts on display are finely woven and embroidered textiles, woodcarvings, weapons, ceramics and Byzantine icons. The photograph collection includes shots of 19th-century revolutionaries and of Agios Nikolaos at the start of the 20th century, showing the port before the advent of tourism.

✚ 138 C3 🍽 Harbour cafés and tavernas (€–€€€) 🚌 Regular service to Iráklio, Malia, Limin Hersónisou, Sitia and Ierapetra 🛳 Services to Sitia, Piraeus, Milos, Santorini, Karpathos, Kassos, Kas, Rhodes and other islands

ℹ Odós Akti I Koundourou 20 ☎ (284101) 22357

**Archiologiko Mouseio**

✉ Odós Palaioíogou 68 ☎ (28410) 24943 🕓 Tue–Sun 8:30–3 ✋ Moderate; free on Sun and national hols from Nov–Mar 🍽 Taverna Aouas (€€)

**Mouseio Laographiko**

✉ Ground floor of Harbour Master's Office, opposite the bridge ☎ (28410) 25093 🕓 Apr–Oct daily 10–4 ✋ Moderate

# a walk in Agios Nikolaos

This walk begins at the harbour in the centre of the resort.

*From the harbour walk up the tamarisk-lined Odós Roussou Koundoúrou, one of the two main shopping streets. Take the first street to the left, Odós Sfakianáki.*

Towards the far end of Odós Sfakianáki there are splendid views of the Gulf of Mirampéllou. The marina below was constructed in 1994.

*At the end of the street, turn left to climb some steps, then make your way down to the waterfront. Here, turn left, passing Kitroplatía Beach, and continue along the waterfront until you come to the harbour.*

Soak up the atmosphere of the harbour with a drink in one of the waterside cafés. The boats and cruisers moored here offer fishing, swimming and glass-bottom boat trips, excursions to Spinalonga Island, (➤ 75) and evening tours of the bay.

*Make for the bridge on the west corner of the harbour and the small Folk Museum (➤ 68). Walk up the steep Odós Palaiológou for a visit to the Archaeological Museum (➤ 67), then retrace your steps down to the lake on your right.*

The 64m (210ft) deep Lake Voulisméni, encircled by fishing boats and flanked by cliffs on its western side, was originally believed to be bottomless. In 1867 it was linked to the harbour by a channel and cleared of its stagnant waters. Today it is a tourist magnet, the lakeview cafés luring customers with their tempting range of exotic ices and cocktails. For the best views climb the steps at the far side, beyond the Café du Lac.

**Distance** 1.8km (1 mile)
**Time** 2 hours (including sights)
**Start Point** Harbour
**End Point** Lake Voulisméni
**Lunch** Taverna Pelagos (€€) ✉ Korakai and Katehaki
☎ (28410) 25737

### DIKTEO ANDRO (DÍKTAEAN CAVE)

According to myth, the Díktaean Cave was the birthplace of Zeus. His father, Kronos, who feared being overthrown by a son, consumed the first five of his offspring. However, when Zeus was born, his mother Rhea presented Kronos with a stone instead of a baby and Zeus was concealed inside the cave, protected by warriors and fed by a goat. As a small child, he was then transferred to the Ídaean Cave (➤ 100).

The actual cave is impressive, but the site is highly commercialized and crowded. Beware of greedy car park attendants, costly donkey rides and persistent guides. Non-slippery shoes are essential. There are now concrete steps and lighting to help you negotiate the 65m (213ft) descent, but unless you are hiring a guide you may want to bring a torch to better examine the cave's natural features more closely.

The cave is a kilometre up from the car park, via a steep, stepped path. An expensive donkey ride is the easy alternative. If you happen to arrive before the tour crowds, the dark cave, with its stalactites and stalagmites, is highly atmospheric. Down in the depths,the venue of ancient cult ceremonies, guides point out the chamber where Zeus was born, and features such as the face of Kronos and a stalagmite in the shape of Rhea and Zeus. Altars, idols and a large number of pottery and bronze votive offerings were found within the cave, some dating back to a pre-Minoan era.

✚ 138 D1 ✉ Psychró, Lasithiou ☎ (29770) 364335 🕐 Daily 8–6:45, 8:30–3 in winter 👋 Moderate 🍴 Tavernas (€€) at the entrance or in the village 🚌 Limited service from Iráklio and from Agios Nikolaos

## ELOUNDA AND SPINALONGA

Thanks to a stunning setting and a choice of luxury hotels Elounda is one of Crete's most desirable resorts. It lies north of Agios Nıkolaos, reached by a road which snakes its way above the Gulf of Mirampéllou, then drops scenically down to the centre of the resort. Life here focuses on the cafés and tavernas around the boat-filled harbour, and the long sandy beach stretching beyond.

Coming into the resort from Agios Nikolaos, a sharp right turning off the main road leads to a causeway linking Elounda to the Spinalonga peninsula. From here you can see the submerged remains of Venetian salt pans. The sunken remnants of the Graeco-Roman city state of Oloús lie towards the end of the causeway to the right of the peninsula. The remains are barely visible but the peninsula is a pleasant place to stroll, with coastal paths and birdlife. A path beside the Canal Bar (just across the bridge) leads to a Byzantine mosaic featuring fish and geometric designs – this is all that remains of an early Christian basilica. Elounda's luxury accommodation, including Crete's finest hotel (Elounda Beach) is situated away from the centre, off the road going south to Agios

Nikolaos. In peaceful surroundings, the hotels have their own private beaches and take full advantage of the glorious views over the gulf.

The rocky island of Spinalonga, reached by *caïque*, lies off shore and is dominated by its Venetian fortress, built in 1579 to protect the port of Elounda. A resistance movement operated here and it was not until 1715, 46 years after the Turkish conquest of the rest of Crete, that the fort finally surrendered. In 1903 the island was turned into a leper colony, where conditions were cruel and prison-like until the construction of a hospital in 1937. Twenty years later the colony was closed and the patients were taken to an Athens hospital.

Today the island is uninhabited and the fortress and town are in ruins.

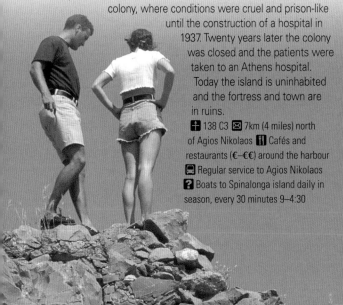

➕ 138 C3 ✉ 7km (4 miles) north of Agios Nikolaos 🍴 Cafés and restaurants (€–€€) around the harbour 🚌 Regular service to Agios Nikolaos ❓ Boats to Spinalonga island daily in season, every 30 minutes 9–4:30

## GOURNIA

The ruins of the Minoan town of Gournia sprawl over the hillside, just off the main Agios Nikolaos–Sitia coastal road. The site is remarkably extensive, and the excavations revealed a thriving Minoan trading town of winding alleys lined by tiny houses, workshops, a marketplace and, on top of the hill, a palace, believed to have belonged to the local ruler or governor. The palace was originally three storeys high, with pillars, courtyards, storerooms and apartments. In relation to Knossos and Phaestos this was something of a mini palace, and the people who lived in the town were probably quite humble in comparison to those of the more famous establishments. Like the other Minoan sites of Crete, Gournia was destroyed in 1450BC, then virtually abandoned. Many finds are housed in the Archaeological Museum in Iráklio (➤ 24–25) and a few in the museum at Sitia (➤ 84–85). If the site is closed, there is a good view from the lay-by next to the entrance track.

✚ 138 U4 ✉ 19km (12 miles) southeast of Agios Nikolaos ☎ (28410) 24943
🕓 Tue–Sun 8:30–7 (earlier in winter)
🖐 Moderate 🍴 Fish tavernas at Pachiá Ammos (€–€€), 2km (1.2 miles) 🚌 Service to Agios Nikolaos and Sitia

## IERAPETRA

Ierapetra is the most southerly town of Europe, enjoying mild winters and many months of sun, and even in mid-winter people bathe in the sea. Agriculture is the mainstay, with off-season vegetables produced in the ugly plastic greenhouses which surround the town.

Both a workaday town and tourist resort, Ierapetra has a bustling, slightly scruffy centre, a pleasant seafront promenade,

a long grey sand beach and an old Turkish quarter with a mosque and fountain house. Architecturally it is uninspiring, and it has little to show of its past importance as a flourishing trading centre. Under the Dorians this was a leading city of Crete, and during the Roman occupation it saw the construction of temples, theatres and other fine buildings. Evidence of its more recent history is the Venetian fortress guarding the harbour. Built in 1212, and refortified by the Turks, this is used today for cultural events during July and August.

The **Archaiologiko Mouseio (Archaeological Museum)** in the centre has a small collection of local finds from Minoan to Roman times. They are not labelled or described, but an English-speaking custodian can usually help. The museum's showpiece is a Minoan larnax, or clay coffin, from Episkopí, north of Ierapetra, which is decorated with lively hunting scenes.

In high season boats leave from the quayside every morning for the island of Yaidhouronísi (or Chrýsi Island) – a popular excursion for those who want to escape the bustle of the town.

➕ 138 E3 ✉ 35km (22 miles) south of Agios Nikolaos 🚌 Regular service to Agios Nikolaos, Iráklio and Sitia 🍴 Tavernas on the seafront (€–€€)

**Archaiologiko Mouseio**

☎ (28420) 28721 🕐 Tue–Sun 8:30–3 💷 Moderate

### KRITSA

Clinging to the slopes of the Díkti Mountains, Kritsa is a large hill village with fine views over the valley. Crafts are the speciality and shops are hung with rugs, embroidery and other home-made (and foreign) products. So close to Agios Nikolaos and also home to the Panagia Kera (➤ 38–39), this is a popular destination for tour coaches, but despite inevitable commercialism, the village retains much of its charm as a working hill community.

✚ 138 D3 ⊠ 10km (6 miles) southwest of Agios Nikolaos 🍴 Tavernas (€–€€€) 🚌 Several a day from Agios Nikolaos ❓ Re-enactment of Cretan weddings in August

### LASITHIOU PLATEAU

The most visited inland region of Lasithiou, the plateau has a spectacular setting, encircled by the Díktaean peaks. Watered by the melting snow from the mountains, the soil is highly fertile, yielding potatoes, cereal crops, vegetables and fruit. Traditionally the land was irrigated by canvas-sailed windmills – the familiar symbols of Lasithiou – but these have gradually given way to the more efficient (if considerably less picturesque) diesel pumps. A few of the originals survive, and there is a row of ruined stone windmills at the Selí Ambélou Pass which heralds the plateau on its northern side. A circular road skirts the plateau (➤ 88–89), passing through small villages with their simple tavernas and craft shops. To avoid the tour crowds at the Díktaean Cave (➤ 72–73), arrive very early in the morning or leave it until the early evening.

✚ 138 C1 ⊠ Southwest of Agios Nikolaos 🍴 Taverna Kronío, Tzermiádho (€) 🚌 Buses make a circular tour of the plateau, stopping at all villages

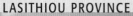

## LATO

The remains of this Dorian town (7th–3rd century BC) occupy a magnificent site, spread on a saddle between two peaks above the Kritsa plain. Relatively few visitors come here, favouring instead the more ancient Minoan sites; but the views alone, encompassing sea and mountains, are worth the visit. The layout of Lato is somewhat simpler than that of the Minoan sites and the extensive ruins, rising in tiers, are notable for the massive stone blocks used in their construction including the entrance gateway, the guard towers, the deep workshops with their wells, the olive presses and the corn-grinding querns. A stepped street with houses and workshops leads up to the central agora – the meeting place and cult centre – with a shrine and a deep rainwater cistern. A broad stairway leads up to two council chambers, lined with benches and two archive rooms. A second stairway leads to a raised terrace with the remains of a temple and altar and a view of the ruined temple on the southeastern hill.

➕ 138 C3 ✉ 3.5km (2 miles) north of Kritsa, 10km west of Agios Nikolaos ⏰ Tue–Sun 8:30–3 💷 Free 🍴 Tavernas in Kritsa (€–€€) 🚌 Buses from Kritsa

## MAKRYGIALOS

With one of the best beaches on Crete's southeast coast, the fishing village of Makrygialos and its sister village Análipsi is a small but growing resort. Hotel development along the main road hides its charms, but head down to the waterfront for a delightful view of its curving sandy beach lined with pleasant tavernas where fresh fish is always on the menu. The shallow water is warm and great for children.

✚ 139 E5 ✉ 24km (15 miles) east of Ierapetra 🍴 Tavernas on the seafront (€–€€) 🚌 Bus service from Ierapetra and Sitia

## MOHLOS

From the main E75 between Agios Nikolaos and Sitia, a minor road snakes down to the fishing village of Mohlos, a peaceful place, with seaside tavernas and a pebble beach. Excavations on the offshore island – once joined to the mainland – revealed the remains of what is believed to be a Minoan harbour town. Finds included ancient seal stones and tombs containing precious vases. A trip to the island can be made with one of the local fishermen (ask at one of the tavernas).

✚ 139 C5 ✉ 40km (25 miles) east of Agios Nikolaos 🍴 Fish tavernas (€–€€) on the seafront 🚌 None

## MONI TOPLOU

Square and solid, the monastery of Toploú lies isolated in the barren hills east of Sitia. Built in the 14th century, it was fortified to resist pirate attacks and named after a large cannon (toploú in Turkish) which was used against invaders. Today it is one of the richest monasteries in Crete. Geared to tourism, the complex may have lost some of its charm as a working monastery, but it certainly merits a visit, particularly for the icons and delightful cobbled courtyard overlooked by three tiers of monks' cells. The most notable of the many icons in the church is the remarkably detailed Lord Thou Art Great (1770), by Ionnis Kornaros. Beyond the church are engravings, icons and a display about the role which the monastery played against the Turks during the Cretan struggle for independence and during World War II.

✚ 139 C7 ✉ 16km (10 miles) east of Sitia ☎ (28430) 61226 🕐 Daily 9–1, 2–6 ✋ Moderate 🍴 Café/snack bar (€) 🚌 Bus service from Sitia then 3km (2 mile) walk from the main road

## NEÁPOLI

A pleasant provincial town and former capital of Lasithiou, Neápoli makes an obvious starting point for an excursion to the Lasithiou Plateau (➤ 78). Few tourists visit the town, but if you are passing by it is worth stopping at one of the cafés or tavernas in the main square to sample the speciality of the town, *soumádha*, a sweet drink made of almonds. A small museum on the square houses crafts and a handful of local archaeological finds.

🔢 138 C2 ✉ 21km (13 miles) northwest of Agios Nikolaos 🍴 Tavernas in the main square (€) 🚌 Regular service from Iráklio and Agios Nikolaos

## PALEKASTRO

Close to the coast and surrounded by olive groves, Palekastro makes a useful base for tourists wanting to explore the sandy beaches, archaeological sites and other attractions at the eastern end of the island. Expanding rapidly, the village has simple hotel accommodation, numerous rooms to rent, a handful of tavernas and bars and even its own tourist office. About 1.5km (1 mile) from the village, near the south end of Chiona beach, lie the partially excavated remains of Roussolakos, one of the largest Minoan towns discovered. Excavations are still in progress and the site – mainly of interest to specialists – is open to the public. Aretefacts from the site are displayed in the archaeological museums of Sitia and Iráklio. There are good sandy beaches to the south of Palekastro, and between the village and Vái to the north. On this stretch of the coast, KGoureménos beach is a good place for windsurfing.

🔢 139 C8 ✉ 18km (11 miles) east of Sitia ✋ Roussolakos free 🍴 Several 🚌 Services from Sitia, Vái and Káto Zakros

ℹ️ Tourist office, Palekastro ☎ (28430) 61546

## PANAGIA KERA

Best places to see ➤ 38–39.

## SITIA

The most easterly town in Crete, at the end of the national highway, Sitia feels quite remote. Both a working port and tourist resort, it is a pleasant, leisurely place, particularly around the taverna-lined quayside and the older streets above the harbour. The town dates back to Graeco-Roman times, possibly even as far back as the Minoan era, but it was under the Venetians that the port had its heyday. Today it is essentially modern, with buildings set in tiers on the hillside. The only evidence of Venetian occupation is the fortress above the bay, reduced to a shell by the Turks, but used now as an open-air theatre. Sitia's long sandy beach, popular with windsurfers, stretches east from the town, followed by the parallel coastal road.

The **Archaiologiko Mouseio (Archaeological Museum),** just out of the centre, has a good collection of

Minoan works of art, with useful explanations in English. Particularly interesting is the section devoted to Zakros Palace (▶ 86–87), with decorated vessels, urns, cooking pots, a wine press and a collection of clay tablets with the rare Linear A script. In the entrance hall pride of place goes to the ivory statuette of

a young man (*c*1450) discovered at Palaíkaistro. The small **Folk Museum,** up from the harbour, has a collection of finely made traditional crafts, including baskets for carrying grapes, and bedspreads and rugs coloured with dye from indigenous plants.

✚ 139 C6 ✉ 70km (43 miles) east of Agios Nikolaos ⑪ Kastro (€€) 🚌 Services from Agios Nikolaos, Iráklio and Ierapetra

**Archaiologiko Mouseio**

✉ Odós Piskokéfalou 3 ☎ (28430) 23917 ⏰ Tue–Sun 8:30–3 💷 Moderate

**Folk Museum**

✉ Odós Kapetán Sífi 28 ☎ (28430) 23917 ⏰ May–Oct Mon–Sat 9:30–1:30 (also Tue and Thu 6–8) 💷 Inexpensive

## VAI BEACH

Backed by a plantation of rare date palms, the tropical-looking Vai beach lies at the northeastern tip of the island. The remote location is no deterrent and the lovely sandy bay is invariably crowded in summer. To see it at its best you must come early in the morning or off-season. Formerly frequented by backpackers, who stayed overnight on the sands, the beach is now strictly regulated, with a camping ban, car park charges and an extensive range of beach facilities.

✚ 139 C8 ✉ 9km (5.5 miles) north of Palekastro ✋ Car park charges
🍴 Taverna (€€) on the beach 🚌 Service to Palekastro and Sitia

## ZAKROS PALACE

Part of the appeal of the Minoan palace of Zakros is the remote valley setting by the coast, seemingly far removed from civilization. However, in Minoan times this was a major centre, linked to a port (now submerged), trading with Egypt

and the Middle East. It wasn't until the 1960s that a Greek professor, Nikolaos Pláton, discovered the palace and its archaeological treasures, their quantity and quality suggesting a highly affluent community.

For an overall view of the setting and layout, start at the upper town; then climb down to the lower level and central court. From here, explore the ceremonial hall, a small banqueting hall and a cluster of other rooms, then cross to the royal apartments. The south side of the central court is bordered by workshops, and in the southeast corner excavators discovered 3,500-year-old olives preserved in water at the bottom of a jar. Treasures from the palace are housed in the Archaeological Museum at Iráklio (➤ 24–25) and Sitia's museum.

🚩 139 D7 ✉ Káto Zakros ☎ (28430) 26897 ⏱ Daily Apr–Oct 8–5; Nov–Mar Tue–Sun 8–3 💷 Moderate; free on Sun in winter 🍴 Maria, Káto Zakros (€) 🚌 Twice a day in summer

# a drive around Lasithiou Plateau

The tour starts from Neápoli but can also be approached from Agios Nikolaos or the north coast. Take non-slip shoes and a torch for the caves.

*Follow the sign for Lasithiou from the main square in Neápoli. The road twists its way scenically up through the mountains.*

Stop at the café at Zénia for a break from the bends and a breathtaking view of the Díktaean peaks.

*Continue up through villages where locals sell wine, rakí and honey by the roadside.*

After about 27km (17 miles), the plateau comes suddenly and spectacularly into view. Stop by the roadside to look down on to the flat plain, encircled by soaring mountains.

*After the village of Mesa Lasithiou, turn right at the road junction for Tzermiádho (signposted to Dzermido).*

Signed from the main road, the Krónio Cave (also known as the Cave of Trápeza) was used as a burial site from prehistoric times. Around 1km (0.6 miles) from the parking area, there are (optional) guides to show you the way.

*Continue along the road encircling the plateau. At the junction at Pinakianó go straight on, following signs for Psychró. Beyond the village of Pláti, follow signs for the Díktaean Cave.*

This is Crete's most famous cave (➤ 72–73), the so-called birthplace of Zeus.

Continue around the plateau until you reach the village of Agios Geórgios which has a folk museum, well signed from the centre.

*At Agios Konstantínos the full circle of the plateau has been completed. Turn right to return to Neápoli.*

**Distance** 83km (51 miles)
**Time** 6–7 hours, including stops and lunch
**Start/End Point** Neápoli 🚩 138 C2
**Lunch** Taverna Kronio (€) ✉ Tzermiádho ☎ (28440) 22375

# Rethymno Province

**Rethymno is the smallest and
most mountainous of Crete's
four provinces. To the east it is
bordered by the towering
peaks of the Psoloreitis
range, to the west by the
Levká Ori or White Mountains.
Between the two lies the beautiful
green Amári Valley, where mountain
hamlets seem lost in time. On the north
coast the main attraction is the delightful historic
town of Rethymno.**

Rethymno

Sandy beaches stretch either side of the provincial capital, and
the coast to the east is built up with a long ribbon of tourist
development. South coast development is restricted by the wild
coastline of cliffs and headlands, and some bays are accessible
only on foot or by dirt track. Agia Galini and Plakias are – for the
moment – the only two resorts developed for package holidays.
The main cultural attractions are the famous monasteries of Arkádi
and Preveli.

### RETHYMNO TOWN

Rethymno was a town of little significance until the
16th and 17th centuries when it prospered under the
Venetians. Following the fall of Constantinople, many
Byzantine scholars sought refuge here and the town
became an important intellectual and cultural centre. In
1646 it came under Turkish rule, which lasted 250 years.
The old quarter retains much of its Venetian and Turkish
character and the town is still regarded as the
'intellectual capital' of the island.

The dominant feature of the town is the mighty
Venetian fortress, built to defend the city against
pirate attacks. To the east lies the harbour, where the
waterside fish tavernas are a magnet for tourists. The
narrow, pedestrianized alleys of the old town are ideal
for strolling. Down virtually every street there are
fascinating architectural details to admire, such as
ornately carved Venetian doorways and arches, the
Turkish overhanging wooden balconies and the minarets

and domes. Tiny shops are crammed with objets d'art, craftsmen sell leather or jewellery, grocery stores are stocked with herbs, spices and rakí. At the end of a morning's stroll head for the Rimondi Fountain, select from one of the surrounding al fresco cafés and watch the world go by.

The town has a wide sandy beach, backed by a palm-lined promenade and tavernas, hotels and cafés. The sands are packed in summer, but there are quieter beaches with cleaner waters away to the east and west.

✚ 134 D3

### Archaiologiko Mouseio (Archaeological Museum)

Occupying the former Turkish prison at the entrance to the

fortress, this is now a modern, well-organized museum of Minoan and Graeco-Roman finds from the Rethymno region. Especially noteworthy are the grave goods and decorated sarcophagi from the late Minoan period, some of them embellished with hunting scenes.

✚ 142 A2 ✉ Fortetza
☎ (28310) 54668
🕐 Tue–Sun 8:30–3
✋ Moderate

### Fortetza (Venetian Fortress)

At the far end of the promontory, above the town, the Venetian fortress was built in 1573–86 to stem the fearsome Turkish attacks on the city. Believed to be the largest Venetian fort ever built, it was designed to protect the entire population of the town. When the Turks attacked in 1646, the Venetian troops took cover here, along with several thousand townspeople; but after a siege of just 23 days, the fortress surrendered. Today the outer walls are well preserved, but most of the buildings were destroyed by earthquakes or by bombs in World War II. Inside the walls the dominant feature is a mosque built for the Turkish garrison, now

restored. Only ruins survive from the garrison quarters, the governor's residence, powder magazines and other buildings, but the atmosphere is evocative and there are fine views. Plays and concerts take place here during the summer months.

✚ 142 A1 ✉ Odós Katecháki ☎ (28310) 28101 ⏰ Tue–Sun 9–6; longer hours in summer ✋ Moderate 🍴 Café (€)

### Kentro Sígkronis Ekastikis Dimiorgeas Rethimnis (Centre of Contemporary Art)

This modern art centre is also known as the L Kanakakis Gallery. The stylish whitewashed galleries on two floors host temporary exhibitions of modern painting, sculpture and other media, mainly by Greek artists. It also has a collection of Greek art, including 70 paintings by Lefteris Kanakakis, a local artist.

**www.rca.gr**

✚ 142 B3 ✉ Odós Chimárras ☎ (28310) 52530 ⏰ Apr–Oct Tue–Fri 9–1, 7–10, Sat and Sun 11–3; Nov–Mar Tue–Fri 9–2, Wed and Fri 6–9, Sat–Sun 10–3 ✋ Moderate

### Mouseio Istorias Kai Laikis Technis (Historical and Folk Museum)

The museum moved in 1995 from its previous site in Mesolongiou to the more spacious setting of a finely restored Venetian house, with a garden, near the Nerantziés Mosque. The galleries house a charming collection of crafts from local homes, including fine embroidery, lace, basketware, pottery, knives and agricultural tools. Explanations, translated into English, accompany displays of bread-making techniques, Greek needlework and other traditional rural crafts.

➕ 142 B2 ✉ Odós Vernardóu ☎ (28310) 23398 ✪ Mon–Sat 9–2, 6–8; Wed, Fri 9–2 in winter 🖐 Moderate 🍴 Cafés and tavernas in Plateía Petiháki (€–€€)

### Temenos Nerantze (Neratziés Mosque)

South of the Rimondi Fountain, the three-domed mosque's finest feature is its soaring minaret. Originally the Church of Santa Maria, it was converted into a mosque by the Turks shortly after their defeat of Rethymno. The minaret was added in 1890 and, prior to closure for safety reasons, afforded splendid views of the town. Today the mosque is a music school and concert hall.

➕ 142 B3 ✉ Odós Vernadóu 28–30 ☎ (28310) 23398 ✪ Closed to public except for concerts 🍴 Cafés and tavernas in Plateía Petiháki (€–€€)

## More to see in Rethymno Province

### AGIA GALINI

At the foot of the Amári valley, with houses, hotels and apartments stacked up on the hillside, Agia Galini has grown from a remote fishing village into a fully fledged tourist resort. The lively, narrow streets of the centre lead down to a harbour of fishing boats and pleasure cruisers and are packed with tavernas, bars and souvenir shops. It is a friendly, cheerful place, but it can become claustrophobic in high season and there is an alarming amount of further construction on the way. The resort beach of stony, dark grey sand to the east of the village is not ideal but there are boats to the more attractive beaches of Agíos Geórgios and Agíos Pávlos to the west, and daily cruises to the sandy beaches of the Paximádia Islands, 12km (7 miles) off shore,

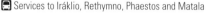 

104 E4 📷 54km (30 miles) southeast of Rethymno 🍴 Onar (€€)
🚌 Services to Iráklio, Rethymno, Phaestos and Matala

## ANOGIA

Lying below the peaks of the Psoloreitis range, Anogia is the last village before the Ídaean Cave, and the main starting point for the hike up to the summit. The village is best known for its crafts, particularly handwoven blankets, rugs, wall hangings and embroidery, all of which you will see on display in the shops. Women at their looms give the village the air of a long-established settlement, but while old traditions survive, all the buildings are new. During World War II, General Kreipe, Commander-in-Chief of the German forces, was kidnapped by partisans and hidden in Anogia, before being removed from Crete. In retaliation the Germans destroyed the entire village, apart from the church, and killed many of the menfolk.

➕ 135 D6 ✉ 35km (22 miles) west of Iráklio 🍽 A couple of simple tavernas (€) in the village 🚌 Service from Iráklio and Rethymno

## BALI

On the north coast, east of Rethymno, Bali is a small but growing resort of rocky coves and tiny sand and shingle beaches. The one-time fishing village is now built up with hotels and apartments, and life here centres primarily on tavernas, bars and discos. Paradise Beach (also known as Evita Beach) is the best place to swim, but the beach is incredibly crowded in summer. Apart from watersports and boat trips to Rethymno there is not a great deal to do here, but Bali is situated roughly half-way between Iráklio and Rethymno, and only 2km (1.2 miles) from the national highway, so there are plenty of opportunities for excursions.

➕ 135 C5 ✉ 30km (19 miles) east of Rethymno 🍽 Harbourside tavernas (€–€€) 🚌 2km (1.2 miles) from bus stop for service to Iráklio and Rethymno

## MONI ARKAIOU

Best places to see ➤ 34–35.

### MONI PREVELI

Best places to see ➤ 36–37.

### ÓROS PSOLOREITIS (MOUNT PSOLOREITIS)

At 2,456m (8,056ft), Mount Psoloreitis, or Mount Ída, is the highest point on Crete. From Anogia (➤ 99) a winding road through barren, mountainous terrain leads to the Nída Plateau at the foot of the mountain. Near the end of the road, by the taverna, a path leads up to the Idaiki Spiliá (Ídaean Cave), a contender, along with the Díktaean Cave (➤ 72–73), for the title of birthplace of Zeus. Excavations in the 1000s yielded bronze shields from the 9th and 8th centuries BC, suggesting that the cave was a post-Minoan cult centre. You can walk down into the cave, but it is fairly shallow with no dramatic natural rock formations. The path to the summit of Mount Psoloreitis also starts at the taverna – a gruelling 7–8 hour return trip.

➕ 135 E5 ✉ 17km (11 miles) south of Anogia to base of mountain

## PLAKIAS

A rapidly expanding resort, Plakias' main asset is its setting, with a long sweep of beach surrounded by steep mountains. It is a fairly low-key place with hotels and apartments, a couple of discos and several beach tavernas with lovely views of the sunset. The beach of shingle and coarse sand is rather exposed, but there's a better one at Damnóni, reached by car or a 30-minute walk.

✚ 134 E2 ✉ 22km (17 miles) southwest of Spíli 🚍 Regularly to Rethymno

## PREVELI BEACH

The beautiful sandy cove at the mouth of the Kourtalióti Gorge can be reached by boat or by a steep and demanding walk from Moni Preveli (► 36–37). It is also known as Palm Beach, after the date palms that line the banks of the River Megapótomos, which flows into the sea at Preveli. Idyllic off-season, the beach fills to overflowing with boatloads of tourists in the summer.

✚ 134 F3 ✉ 38km (24 miles) south of Rethymno 🚢 Day trips from Plakias and Agia Galini

## SPILAIO TOU MELIDONI (MELIDONI CAVE)

Mythical home of Talos, the bronze giant who guarded the coasts of Crete, the Melidoni Cave has some splendid stalactites and stalagmites. But it is not so much the natural beauty of the cave as its tragic history that has earned it fame. In 1824 around 370 of the villagers, mostly women, children and the elderly, hid here from the Turks. Troops laid siege to the cave but the villagers refused to surrender and shot two of the enemy. In retaliation the Turks blocked the entrance of the caves, trying to suffocate the Cretans. Then they lit fires at the cave mouth, asphyxiating everyone inside. An ossiary in one of the chambers still contains the victims' bones, and an annual commemoration service is held in the local church.

✚ 135 D5 ✉ 4km (2.5 miles) northeast of Pérama, a short drive or 30 minutes' walk from the village of Melidoni ☎ (28340) 22046 🕐 Apr–Nov daily 9–6:30/7 💷 Moderate 🍴 Bar by the cave (€)

# Amári Valley

*a drive*

Dwarfed on the east side by the Psoloreitis massif, the fertile Amári valley offers glorious views.

*From Rethymno head east on the old national highway, turning right at the sign for Amári. At the village of Agia Fotinís go straight on, then turn left for Thrónos.*

Thrónos has a lovely church with medieval frescoes and an early Byzantine mosaic pavement. (Ask locally for the key if the church is locked.) Beyond the church a path leads up to the ruins of the ancient city of Sybrito.

*Return to the main road and continue to Moní Asomáton where Venetian monastery buildings are occupied by an agricultural college. After another 2km (1.2 miles) turn right for Amári (5km/3 miles).*

Amári has wonderful valley views and some faded frescoes in the Church of Agia Ánna.

*Returning to the main road, turn right for Vizári which has Roman and Byzantine remains. After Nithavris (11km/ 7 miles) take the road east to Zarós (24km/15 miles)*

An attractive mountain village, Zarós is famous for its springs. Stop for lunch at one of the tavernas serving trout.

*Return towards Rethymno, this time taking the road on the west side of the valley, to reach Gerakári.*

Gerakári is famous for its cherry trees, and you can buy bottled cherries and cherry brandy in the village. At Méronas, 4km (2.5 miles) beyond Gerakári, admire the views across the valley and the frescoes in Panagia church.

*Back at Agia Fotínis, turn left to return to Rethymno.*

**Distance** 165km (102 miles)
**Time** With stops and lunch allow a full day
**Start/End Point** Rethymno ✚ 134 D3
**Lunch** Taverna Votomos (€€) ✉ Zarós ☎ (28940) 31302

# Hania Province

**The most westerly province
in Crete, Hania has no great
archaeological sites but it
provides some of the most
spectacular scenery on the
island. Views are dominated by the
majestic peaks of the Levká Óri (White
Mountains), snow-capped for six months of
the year. On the south coast the mountains
drop abruptly to the Libyan Sea, leaving little
space for any major development.**

Hania

Compared to the flatter north coast, the south is sparsely
populated, with just a handful of villages nestling below the
mountains and a couple of holiday resorts with beaches.
Spectacular, walkable gorges are a feature of the White
Mountains, particularly the Samaria Gorge, which is the second
most popular attraction in Crete. On the north coast the historic
town of Hania, which incorporates the island's most beautiful
harbour, makes a delightful base.

### HANIA TOWN

The ancient city of Kydonía, inhabited since neolithic times, became the most important settlement in Crete after the destruction of Knossos. The town fell into decline under the Arabs, but during the Venetian occupation (1290–1646) La Canea, as it was renamed, became 'the Venice of the East'. Following the Turkish occupation, which was from 1646–1898, Hania was made capital of Crete and remained so until 1971.

Hania is not only the best base for exploring western Crete, it is arguably the island's most appealing town. Beautifully set below the White Mountains, it has a lively harbour, a maze of alleys and a string of beaches nearby. Strolling is the most pleasurable activity, either along the harbourfront, or through the streets of the old town, where Venetian and Turkish houses have been elegantly restored. Along the narrow alleys are such charming features as old portals and overhanging balconies, as well as enticing hole-in-the-wall craft shops and cafés.

The real magnet is the outer harbour, with its faded, shuttered houses, and its crescent of cafés and tavernas overlooking the water. This is where the locals come for their early evening vólta. The inner harbour, overlooked by Venetian arsenals, is another focal point, with fishing boats, pleasure craft and tavernas. Hania may be picturesque, but there are often too many tourists

crowding the narrow streets. To appreciate its
beauty, visit early or later in the day.
✚ 133 B5

### Archaiologiko Mouseio
### (Archaeological Museum)

The Church of St Francis was the largest church to
be built in Hania during the Venetian era, and its spacious vaulted
interior makes a handsome setting for the archaeological
discoveries from excavations in the region. The exhibits span the
period from late neolithic to Roman occupation,
and greatly assist in adding a human dimension
to the ancient sites of the area.

The majority of artefacts date from the late
Minoan era and include pottery, weapons, seals,
decorated clay tombs *(larnakes)* and tablets
inscribed with Linear A and B scripts. The
Graeco-Roman section is represented by a
collection of sculpture and glassware, leading
up to three fine Roman mosaics, which were
discovered in villas in Hania, displayed at the
far end of the church.

The little garden beside the church features
a damaged Lion of St Mark, and a beautifully
preserved ten-sided Turkish fountain, dating from
the period when the church was converted by
the Turks into a base of a minaret.

✚ 142 E2 ✉ Odós Khalídon, 21 ☎ (28210) 90334
🕐 Summer Mon 1–7:30, Tue–Sun 8:30–7:30; winter
Mon 1–5, Tue–Fri 8:30–5, Sat–Sun 8:30–3 💷 Moderate
🍴 Tavernas in Odós Khalídon or on the harbour (€–€€€)

### Hania Limani (Hania Harbour)
Best places to see ➤ 30–31.

## Mouseio Nautiko (Naval Museum)

Tracing Crete's sea trade and maritime warfare, the Naval Museum is housed in the restored Venetian Fírkas Tower guarding Hania's harbour. Most of the exhibits here are models of ships, ranging from the simple craft of the Copper Period (2800BC) to submarines built in the 1980s. The collection also contains marine weapons and instruments, historical documents, a model of the Venetian town of La Canea and, on the first floor, an exhibition devoted to the World War II Battle of Crete in 1941. Beyond the gate, the strategically sited bastion commands impressive views of the harbour, the Venetian lighthouse and the domed Mosque of the Janissaries (built in 1645, following the Turkish conquest). It was here, at the Fírkas fortifications, that the Greek flag was first raised on Crete in November 1913.

➕ 142 D2 ✉ Fort Fírkas, Aktí Kountourioti ☎ (28210) 26437 🕐 Daily 9–4; 10–2 in winter ✋ Moderate

## Vizantino Mouseio (Byzantine Museum)

Hania's newest museum is in a small, renovated church on the western side of the fortress. Its displays incorporate a range of Byzantine artefacts, including mosaics, sculptures and jewellery as well as the usual collection of icons. A highlight is the icon of St George slaying the dragon, at the far end of the musem. It was painted by Emmanuel Tzanes Bouniales (1610–90), one of the foremost arists of the Cretan school of icon painters. Particularly oustanding are the brightly coloured fragments of 11th-century wall frescoes. The San Salvatore collection, in a well-lit side gallery, includes a beautiful display of glass bead necklaces, jewellery, crosses, ceramics, Byzantine coins and a rare bronze lamp from the 6th and 7th centuries. There are also some fascinating post-Byzantine artefacts, such as the curious horned mask from 16th–17th century Hania town.

➕ 142 D2 ✉ Odós Theotokopoulou, 82 ☎ (28210) 96046 🕐 Mon 12–7, Tue–Fri 8:30–7, Sat–Sun 8:30–3 ✋ Moderate; free on Sun in winter

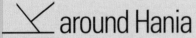

# around Hania

Start at the Naval Museum (➤ 109), which is situated on the west side of the Old Harbour.

*With the water on your right, walk along the exterior of the fortifications and cut inland along Odós Theotokopoúlou, a picturesque street with old Venetian houses and craft shops. At the end, turn left down Odós Zambelioú and at the main square turn right.*

Odós Halídon, lined with shops, is the tourist hub of Hania. On the right is the Archaeological Museum (➤ 107) and just beyond it, in the courtyard of the Catholic church, the small Folk Museum. On the other side of the road lie the Turkish Baths and a large square, overlooked by Hania's unremarkable cathedral.

*Take the second left for Odós Skridlóf, a narrow alley packed with leather stalls, and go straight on for the covered market. Continuing along the same road, take the second street on the left for the delightful 16th-century Agíos Anárgyroi, housing ancient icons.*

At end of the street the tree-lined Plateia 1821 is overlooked by Agios Nikolaos, a former mosque which retains its soaring minaret.

*At the opposite side of the square turn right for the Inner Harbour. Divert left along Odós Karneváro to see the*

Greek/Swedish excavations which have revealed Minoan remains.

At the waterfront, on the right, are the vaults of the 16th century Venetian Arsenal. Fish tavernas overlook the colourful Inner Harbour. From here you can walk along the jetty to the lighthouse, or turn left to return to the Old Harbour, passing the Mosque of the Janissaries.

**Distance** 2.5km (1.5 miles)
**Time** 2–3 hours including sightseeing
**Start/End Point** Venetian Harbour ✚ 142 D2
**Lunch** Dinos (€€€) ✉ Aktí Enóseas 3, Inner Harbour
☎ (28210) 41865

## More to see in Hania Province

### ELAFONISI

The semi-tropical beach of Elafonisi is one of the finest in the whole of Crete, with its pink-tinged sands and vivid turquoise waters. The beach is remotely located in the southwest of the island and visitors who wish to reach it by car face a long drive and many hairpin bends.

However, it is no longer the undiscovered and idyllic haven it used to be – there are now several restaurants, two small hotels, rooms to rent and, in high season, tourist boats and buses crammed full with eager daytrippers. A more peaceful alternative to the main beach is the tiny island of Elafonisi, just offshore, which is reached by wading knee-deep through the turquoise waters. Here there is another idyllic beach, where the waters are clear, shallow and ideal for children.

✚ 132 E2 ✉ 6km (4 miles) south of Chrysoskalítissas ⒤ Several cafés and tavernas (€–€€) 🚌 Once a day from Hania ⛴ Ferries from Paleohora

### FALASSARNA

As you wind down the hillside to the west coast, Falassarna's magnificent swooping beach comes into view, its crescent of pale sands, lapped by azure waters, stretching round to Cape Koutrí in the north.

Falassarna is also the site of an ancient city, the remains of which can be seen 2km (1 mile) north of the beach. (Follow

the track for 1.5km/1 mile beyond the last building.) Among the scattered remnants of the Hellenistic city-state are a 'throne' carved out of the rock, tombs, quarries, towers, water cisterns and the ruins of houses and storerooms. The remains centre around the harbour basin, its location some 100m (328ft) inland showing clear evidence of the gradual shifting of the island. In the distant past Crete's west coast was uplifted by 6–9m (20–30ft), while parts of eastern Crete were submerged, including the sunken city of Oloús (► 74). Excavations of the ancient city are still in the early stages, and only a small portion of the harbour has been unearthed.

More remains lie at the top of Cape Koutrí, site of the acropolis. Close by, the less appealing – but economically necessary – plastic greenhouses produce off-season vegetables which are exported to mainland Greece.

➕ 132 B2 ✉ 8km (5 miles) northwest of Plátanos ✋ No charge to see the ruins
🍴 2 tavernas above the beach (€–€€)
🚌 2 per day from Hania

### FARANGI IMBROU (IMPROS GORGE)

North of Hóra Sfakión, the Impros Gorge is a small-scale version of the famous Samaria Gorge (➤ 26–27). Not quite as spectacular but with similar scenery, it is far more peaceful than Samaria. The gorge is about 8km (5 miles) long, and the walk takes from 2 to 3 hours, either uphill from the coast east of Hóra Sfakión, or downhill from Impros village at the beginning of the gorge. At the end you either have to walk to Hóra Sfakión, catch a bus or wait for a taxi in Komitádes. The walk can only be made between May and October since winter torrents render the gorge impassable.

✚ 133 E7 ✉ 54km (33 miles) southeast of Hania ♨ Free 🍴 Café (€) in Impros 🚌 Service from Hania and Hóra Sfakión ❓ Sturdy footwear and drinks recommended

### FARANGI SAMARIAS (SAMARIA GORGE)

Best places to see ➤ 26–27.

### FRANGOKASTELLO

The great square fortress, formidable from a distance, is actually no more than a shell. It was built by the Venetians in 1340 in an attempt to subdue the rebellious Sfakiots and the pirates who were attacking Crete from the African coast. In 1770 the Sfakiot rebel leader, Daskaloyiánnis, was forced to surrender to the Turks here, and in 1828, during the Greek War of Independence, the Greek leader, Hatzimicháli Daliánis, along with several hundred Cretans, died defending the fort against the Turks. According to the locals, on the anniversary of the massacre in mid-May their ghosts appear at dawn and march around the walls.

Below the fortress there is excellent swimming and snorkelling from the sandy beach, and there are tavernas, shops, rooms to rent and even a disco. Less crowded beaches lie to the east and west.

🚹 133 F7 ✉ 17km (11 miles) east of Hóra Sfakión 🔳 Free 🍽 Several tavernas (€–€€) 🚌 Limited service to Hóra Sfakión and Plakias

### GAVDOS

A remote island between Crete and the shores of northern Africa, Gavdos is the southernmost point in Europe. A few families eke

out a living here and there are some rooms to rent and a couple of basic tavernas. The landscape is somewhat desolate and sunbaked, but for those prepared to walk there are some beautiful, unspoilt beaches. Ferries (which can take several hours if the seas are choppy) arrive at Karabe; from here you walk for half an hour to the nearest beach or climb for an hour up to Kastrí, the main village on the island. Sometimes visitors can get transport from locals meeting the ferries.

🚹 132 F2 (inset) ✉ 48km (30 miles) south of Hóra Sfakión 🍽 Limited choice (€) 🚢 Ferries from Palaeochora and Hóra Sfakión

# a walk through the Samaria Gorge

Start at the tourist pavilion at the head of the gorge. Hikers should come equipped with sturdy footwear, sunhat, sunscreen and refreshments (there are drinking points and streams along the gorge but no food).

*Take the stairway known as the xilóskala (wooden stairs) which drops steeply, descending 1,000m (3,280ft) in the first 2km (1 mile).*

The first landmark is the tiny Church of Agíos Nikolaos, shaded by pines and cypresses.

*The path narrows as you reach the bottom of the gorge (4km/2.5 miles from the start). In summer the river is reduced to a mere trickle.*

The half-way point, and a good spot for a picnic, is the abandoned village of Samaria. The inhabitants were rehoused when the area became a national park. To the east of the gorge lies the small 14th-century Church of Óssia María, containing original frescoes. The church gave its name to the village and gorge.

*Follow the narrowing trail between towering cliffs, crossing the river at various points. Continue walking until you see a small church on the left.*

Beyond the sanctuary built by the Sfakiots, you can see ahead the famous *sideróportes* or Iron Gates. The corridor narrows to a mere 3m (10ft), the towering walls either side rising to 300m (984ft).

*Beyond the gates, the path opens out and you walk down the valley to the coast.*

At the old abandoned village of Agia Rouméli, a drinks kiosk is a welcome sight.

*Continue to the modern coastal village of Agía Rouméli where tavernas, the cool sea water and the ferry back to civilization await.*

**Distance** 16km (10 miles)
**Time** 5–7 hours 🕐 May to mid-Oct (mid-Apr to Oct weather permitting)
**Start point** Omalós Plain, 43km (27 miles) south of Hania ✚ 133 D5 🚌 Service from Hania
**End Point** Agia Rouméli ✚ 133 D5 ⛴ Ferries to Hóra Sfakión, where there are buses back to Hania. Check times of the last boats and buses. Guided tours available through any travel agent
**Lunch** Tavernas at the top of the gorge and in Agia Rouméli (€–€€); a picnic is recommended for the gorge

## GEORGIOUPOLI

This north coast resort was named in honour of Prince George, who became High Commissioner of Crete in 1898, after the Turks were forced to recognize the island's right to autonomy. The fishing village is now a well established resort, with hotels, rooms to rent and a huge sweep of beach, but despite ongoing construction, it is still a relatively peaceful and relaxed place. The eucalyptus trees which shade the large central square are watered by the River Almyróu, which flows into the sea at Georgioupoli. To explore the river, its birdlife, crabs and turtles, you can hire pedaloes or canoes from the little chapel which sits at the end of the causeway. The sandy beach stretches for several kilometres to the east, but beyond the causeway, the strong currents make swimming conditions dangerous.

133 D7 22km (14 miles) west of Rethymno Tavernas on the main square (€–€€) Service to Rethymno and Hania

## HÓRA SFAKIÓN

In the 16th century this was the largest town on the south coast, with a population of 3,000, but rebellions during the Turkish occupation left Hóra Sfakión largely impoverished, and what remained of the town was destroyed by bombs in World War II. Today it is no more than a small resort and ferry port, its main appeal the setting between the mountains and the crystal clear waters of the Libyan Sea. The small pebble beach is not ideal but you can take boats or walk to Sweetwater Beach, which takes its name from the freshwater springs seeping from beneath the rocks. The beach is a popular spot for nudist campers.

In high season the seaside tavernas of Hóra Sfakión cater for boatloads of hungry hikers coming from the Samaria Gorge, waiting for buses back to Hania. The town has always been the capital of this mountainous, remote region and Sfakiots, as the locals are known, are traditionally a proud and independent people. The region was a centre of resistance during the fight for Cretan independence and continued this heroic tradition in World War II, sheltering Allied troops after the Battle of Crete.

✠ 133 E6 ✉ 67km (42 miles) south of Hania 🍴 Seafront tavernas (€–€€) 🚌 Service to Hania and Plakias ⛴ Ferries to Agia Rouméli (Samaria Gorge), Sougia, Palaeochora and the island of Gavdos.

## KISSAMOS

This is a pleasant coastal town, still retaining some of its Cretan character but offering little of architectural interest. Few tourists stay here but there are a couple of hotels and some rooms to rent, many of them by the beach. A new Archaiologiko Mouseio (Archaeological Museum) was opened in 2006 to display local artefacts. The best places to eat are the tavernas on the seafront, where you can also sample the a glass of the locally produced red wine.

✠ 132 B2 ✉ 40km (25 miles) west of Hania 🍴 Papadakis (€) 🚌 Services to Falassarna, Hóra Sfakión, Hania and Palaeochora

## KOLIMBARI AND MONI GONIAS

At the foot of the Rodopoú peninsula, Kolimbari is a pleasantly unspoilt coastal village, where local life goes on undisturbed by the few tourists who stay here. The beach is pebbly but the waters are crystal clear and there are splendid views over the Gulf of Hania.

About 1km (0.6 miles) north of the village the Moni Gonias has a delightful coastal setting. Founded in 1618, it has been rebuilt several times but the Venetian influence can still be seen in some of the architectural features. The small church contains some wonderfully detailed little icons from the 17th century along the top of the iconostatis, as well as votive offerings and other treasures. The most precious icons, dating from the 15th century, are housed in the museum, along with reliquaries and vestments. If the church and museum are closed, ask one of the monks to show you round. He will probably also point out the Turkish cannon ball lodged in the rear wall of the church.

🕇 132 B3 ✉ 23km (14 miles) west of Hania ☎ (28240) 22518 🕐 Sun–Fri 7–12:30, 4–8 (shorter hours in winter) ✋ Free 🍴 Seafront fish tavernas (€–€€) in Kolimbari 🚌 Service to Kolimbari from Hania and Kissamos

### LOUTRO

The only way to get to this delightful, car-free village is on foot or by boat. It is a tiny, remote place, with white cubed houses squeezed between towering mountains and the Libyan sea. There are half a dozen tavernas, a simple hotel, rooms to rent and some villas, but the majority of visitors are daytrippers coming on ferries from Hóra Sfakión and Agia Rouméli. The pebble beach is not ideal but you can bathe from the rocks or hire canoes to explore offshore islets, coves and beaches. There are also boat trips to the sandy cove of Mármara and to Sweetwater Beach.

🕇 133 E6 ✉ 5km (3 miles) west of Hóra Sfakión 🍴 The Blue House (€) 🚢 Ferry service to Hóra Sfakión and Agia Rouméli

### MALEME

The resort of Maleme is part of the long ribbon of modern development west of Hania. But it is for its role in World War II that this part of the coast is best known. It was at the Maleme airstrip that the Germans first landed in their invasion of 1941, the Allied forces retreating from 'Hill 107' above the airstrip. The Germans occupied this strategic target – but not without casualties. Today 'Hill 107' is the location of the German War Cemetery, where nearly 4,500 Germans are buried.

🕇 132 B4 ✉ 16km (10 miles) west of Hania

## MONI CHRYSOSKALITISSAS

In a remote location at the southwest tip of the island, the whitewashed nunnery perches on a promontory above the sea. It was founded in a cave in the 13th century, but the present building dates from the mid-19th century and contains little of interest to the average tourist. Of the 200 sisters who used to live here, just one and a monk remain. For centuries Moni Chrysoskalitissas, its barrel roof a distinctive landmark, was a refuge for victims of shipwrecks on this remote and treacherous coast. The name 'Chrysoskalítissas' means 'Golden Steps', and was taken from the stairway of 90 steps leading from the nunnery down to the sea. According to legend, one of the steps is made of pure gold – but is only recognisable to those who are free of sin!

✚ 132 D1 ✉ 13km (8 miles) southwest of Váthi ☎ (28220) 61261
🕐 7am–sunset 💶 Free 🍴 2 tavernas (€) on the Váthi road

## PALEOCHORA

Formerly a fishing village, and one-time haunt of hippies, Palaeochora now has universal appeal, with its fine setting below rugged mountains, its excellent beaches and relaxed atmosphere. As yet it is free from mass tourism, sitting on a small peninsula, crowned by the stone walls of a Venetian castle. Beneath it are two beautiful bays: to the east a sheltered but shingle and pebble beach, to the west a long stretch of wide golden sands shaded by tamarisk trees and very popular with windsurfers.

Venizélos, the main street, is lively at night, when the road is closed to traffic and taverna tables spill out on to the pavements. Despite its popularity the centre has not lost all its Cretan character – locals still frequent the cafés and fishermen land their catch at the quayside. Linked to coastal villages by a regular ferry service, the resort makes an excellent base for exploring southern Crete, and is well placed for hikers, with coastal and mountain

walks. There are also weekend boats to the tiny island of Gavdos (► 115).

➕ 132 E3 ✉ 80km (50 miles) southwest of Hania 🍴 Tavernas and retaurants (€–€€) 🚌 Regular service to Hania 🚢 Ferries to Sougia, Agía Rouméli, Loutro, Hóra Sfakión and Gavdos ℹ (028230) 41507

### RODOPOÚ PENINSULA

The remote and rugged Rodopoú peninsula extends 18km
(11 miles) from the low lying coast west of Hania. The roads
only go as far as the hamlet of Afráta and the main village of
Rodopoú. Beyond this the peninsula is uninhabited, the access
limited to rough tracks and footpaths. There are good walks in the
mountainous interior, but the tracks can be rough and there is very
little shade. At the northeastern tip of the peninsula lie the scant
Graeco-Roman remains of the Sanctuary of the goddess Diktynna,
excavated by the Germans during World War II. Statues from the
temple, which were discovered here, are now in the Hania
Archaeological Museum (➤ 107). The easiest way to reach the
remains is to take a boat excursion from Hania
or Kolimbari. Part of the attraction is the pretty,
sheltered cove below the sanctuary, ideal for
swimming. Going by car entails a rough ride and
half an hour's walk. On the west coast, the
isolated little Church of Agíos Ioánnis is reached
by a rough, dusty track from Rodopoú, taking
two to three hours. This is the route taken by
thousands of pilgrims every year on 28 and 29
August (St John the Baptist's Day) to witness the
baptism of boys with the name of John (Ioánnis).

✚ 132 A3 ✉ West of Hania Bay 🍴 Simple cafés and tavernas in Afráta and
Rodopoú (€) 🚌 Limited service to the village of Rodopoú

### SOUDA BAY ALLIED WAR CEMETERY

Sheltered by the Akrotíri peninsula to the north, Souda Bay is
Crete's largest natural harbour. Laid out on a neatly tended lawn,
sloping down to the water, are the graves of 1,497 Allied soldiers
who died defending Crete in World War II. The names of the
soldiers, many of whom lie in unknown graves, are listed in the
Cemetery Register, which is kept in a box at the entrance to the
building. Of the total Allied force on the island of 32,000 men,

18,000 were evacuated, 12,000 were taken prisoner and 2,000 were killed.
🚹 133 B5 ✉ 5km (3 miles) southeast of Hania harbour 🚌 Service from Hania to Souda Bay

## SOUGIA

Against the backdrop of the Samaria hills, this former fishing port is rapidly expanding into a tourist resort. Right at the end of a long twisting road from Hania, it was first discovered by backpackers, but more and more tourists are coming for the long pebble beach, translucent blue waters, simple tavernas and coastal and mountain walks. As yet, accommodation is fairly basic. Just to the east of the Soúganos River mouth, a few Roman relics survive from the ancient port, which served the Graeco-Roman city of Elirós, 5km (3 miles) to the north. To the west a fine Byzantine mosaic, now in the Hania Archaeological Museum (➤ 107), was discovered where the modern church stands. Three kilometres to the west of the village, reached by boat or on foot over the cliffs (70–90 minutes) lie the classical Greek and Roman ruins of the ancient city of Lissós.
🚹 132 E4 ✉ 70km (43 miles) southwest of Hania 🍴 Simple tavernas in the resort (€) 🚌 Service from Hania

# a drive around the Akrotíri Peninsula

*From Hania take the airport road, turning left at the top of the hill for the Venizélos Graves.*

Stone slabs mark the graves of Elefthérios Venizélos (1864–1936), Crete's famous statesman and his son, Sophoklís. The site commands a magnificent view of Hania, mountains and coast.

*Continue on the airport road, then follow signs for Agia Triada.*

The Venetian-influenced 17th-century monastery has a church with a fine Renaissance façade, and a peaceful courtyard where cats doze under fruit trees. A small shop sells olive oil made by the monks and a museum houses a collection of icons, reliquaries and vestments.

*From Agia Triada, walk or drive along the track through rocky, barren hills to the Gouvernétou Monastery (4.5km/2.8 miles).*

This sleepy, isolated monastery, founded in 1548, also shows a strong Venetian influence. From the monastery a path (about 30 minutes' walk) leads down to a beautiful gorge with the ruins of Katholikó Monastery and Cave of St John the Hermit. Pilgrims come here on 7 October each year to celebrate the saint's day.

*Retrace the route to Agia Triada, go back towards the airport and after nearly 16km (10 miles) turn right for Chorafákeia (3km/2 miles). At the village turn right for Stavrós.*

The beautiful bay of pale sands and calm, aquamarine waters were the setting scenes in *Zorba the Greek*.

*Return to Chorafákeia and in the village turn right for Hania. Reaching the coast, stop at Kalathás Beach.*

One of the prettiest beaches on the peninsula, this is a good spot for a swim and a meal in a taverna before the return journey to Hania.

**Distance** 45km (28 miles)
**Time** Half a day, including sightseeing
**Start/End point** Hania ✚ 133 B5
**Lunch** Kalathás (€–€€) ✉ Kalathás beach, Kalathás
☎ (28210) 64729

# Index

# Acknowledgements

The Automobile Association would like to thank the following photographers, companies and picture libraries for their assistance in the preparation of this book.

Abbreviations for the picture credits are as follows – (t) top; (b) bottom; (c) centre; (l) left; (r) right; (AA) AA World Travel Library.

4l ferry, AA/K Paterson; 4c Preveli, AA/P Enticknap; 4r Matala, AA/K Paterson; 5l Chania, AA/K Paterson; 5c Cafe, AA/N Hicks; 6/7 Ferry, AA/K Paterson; 10/11 Procession before Easter, AA/P Enticknap; 16 Telephone, AA/N Hicks; 20/21 Monastery complex at Preveli, AA/P Enticknap; 22 Relic from Ayia Triadha Minoan Summer Palace, AA; 22/23t Ayia Triadha, AA/K Paterson; 22/23b Agia Triada, AA/N Hicks; 24 Archaeological Museum in Irakleio, AA/K Paterson; 224/25t Agia Triada in Irakleio, AA/P Enticknap; 24/25b Archaeological Museum, AA/K Paterson; 26 Samaria Gorge, AA/N Hicks; 26/27 Samaria Gorge, AA/N Hicks; 27 Samaria Gorge, AA/N Hicks; 28 Gortys, AA/P Enticknap; 28/29t Gortys, AA/N Hicks; 28/29b Ayios Titos church, AA/P Enticknap; 30 Lighthouse in Chania, AA/N Hicks; 30/31 Harbour of Chanio, AA/P Enticknap; 32 Fresco – Ladies in Blue from Knossos, AA; 32/33t Knosos, AA/N Hicks; 32/33b Knosos, AA/N Hicks; 34/35 Moni Arkadiou Monastery, AA/N Hicks; 35 Moni Arkadiou Monastery, AA/N Hicks; 36/37 Moni Preveli, AA/N Hicks; 37 Moni Preveli, AA/K Paterson; 38 Panagia Kera, AA/K Paterson; 38/39 Panagia Kera, AA/N Hicks; 40 Faistos, AA/N Hicks; 40/41 Kamares wine krater, AA; 41 Minoan Palace at Faistos, AA/P Enticknap; 42/43 Matala, AA/K Paterson; 45 Fodhele, AA/K Paterson; 46 Ayios Minas Cathedral, AA/K Paterson; 45/47 Ayios Minas Cathedral, AA/K Paterson; 48 Agios Marcos, AA/K Paterson; 48/49 Agios Titos, AA/K Paterson; 50/51 Historical Museum, AA/P Enticknap; 51 Historical Museum, AA/K Paterson; 52 Koules Fort, AA/K Paterson; 54 Fodele, AA/N Hicks; 54/55 Shopkeeper in Fodele, AA/K Paterson; 55 Church in Fodele, AA/P Enticknap; 56/57 Hersonissou, GOwst/Alamy; 58/59 Malia, AA/N Hicks; 59 Malia, AA/W Voysey; 60 Matala, AA/K Paterson; 60/61 Matala, AA/K Paterson; 62/63 Voroi, AA/K Paterson; 63 Voroi, AA/P Enticknap; 64 Restaurant, AA/K Paterson; 65 Vai beach, AA/K Paterson; 66/67 Agia Triada Cathedral, AA/N Hicks; 66/67b Ayios Nikolaos, AA/K Paterson; 67 Archaeological Museum, AA/N Hicks; 68 Archaeological Museum, AA/N Hicks; 68/69 Archaeological Museum, AA/N Hicks; 69 Kitro Plateia beach, ?; 70/71 Agios Nikolaos, AA/N Hicks; 71 Agios Nikolaos, AA/N Hicks; 72/73 Diktaean cave, AA/K Paterson; 73 Diktaean cave, AA/K Paterson; 74/75t Spinalogka, AA/K Paterson; 74/75b Spinalogka, AA/K Paterson; 76 Gournia, AA/K Paterson; 76/77 Lerapetra, AA/K Paterson; 77 Lerapetra, AA/K Paterson; 78t Kritsa, AA/N Hicks; 78b Lasithi, AA/K Paterson; 78/79 Lasithiou Plateau, AA/K Paterson; 80 Mochlos, AA/K Paterson; 80/81 Toplou, AA/K Paterson; 81 Toplou, AA/K Paterson; 82 Dikti Mountain, AA/K Paterson; 84/85t Siteia Mountains, AA/K Paterson; 84/85b Siteia, AA/K Paterson; 86/87 Zakros Palace, AA/K Paterson; 88 Lasithiou Plateau, AA/K Paterson; 88/89 Wild Thyme, AA/N Hicks; 89 Diktaean Cave, AA/K Paterson; 90 carnations in Margarites, AA/K Paterson; 91 Rethymno, AA/N Hicks; 92/93t Rethymno, AA/K Paterson; 92/93b Fishing Boats, AA/P Enticknap; 93 Rethymno, AA/N Hicks; 94 Mosque in Venetian fortress in Rethymno, AA/N Hicks; 95 Venetian fortress in Rethymno, AA/K Paterson; 96 Museum of History and Folk Art, AA/K Paterson; 97 Rethymno, AA/K Paterson; 98/99t Agia Galini, AA/N Hicks; 98/99b Agia Galini, AA/K Paterson; 100 Ida Mountains, AA/K Paterson; 100/101 Mount Psilore, AA/P Enticknap; 102/103 Flowers in the Amari Valley, AA/K Paterson; 104 Samaria Gorge, AA/K Paterson; 105 Sougia, AA/K Paterson; 106 Chania, AA/N Hicks; 106/107 Archaeological Museum, AA/P Enticknap; 107 Chania, AA/N Hicks; 108/109 Naval Museum, Chania, AA/N Hicks; 110 Chania, AA/K Paterson; 111t Stall in Chania, AA/N Hicks; 111b Venetian lighthouse, AA/N Hicks; 112/113 Elafonisi, AA/P Enticknap; 114/115 Fragkokastelo, AA/K Paterson; 116 Samaria Gorge, AA/N Hicks; 118 Georgioupoulis, AA/K Paterson; 119 Kasteli Kissamou, AA/K Paterson; 120/121 Moni Gonias monastery, AA/K Paterson; 121 Loutro, AA/K Paterson; 122 Moni Chrysoskalitisss, AA/K Paterson; 122/123t Taverna, AA/K Paterson; 122/123b Palaiochora, AA/K Paterson; 124/125 Rodopou Peninsula, AA/K Paterson; 125 Mosaic in church in Sougia, AA/K Paterson; 126 Akrotiri Peninsula, AA/P Enticknap; 126/127 Gouverneto Monastery, AA/K Paterson; 127 Tomb of Venizelos, Profitis Ilias, AA/P Enticknap.

Every effort has been made to trace the copyright holders, and we apologise in advance for any accidental errors. We would be happy to apply the corrections in the following edition of this publication.

# Maps

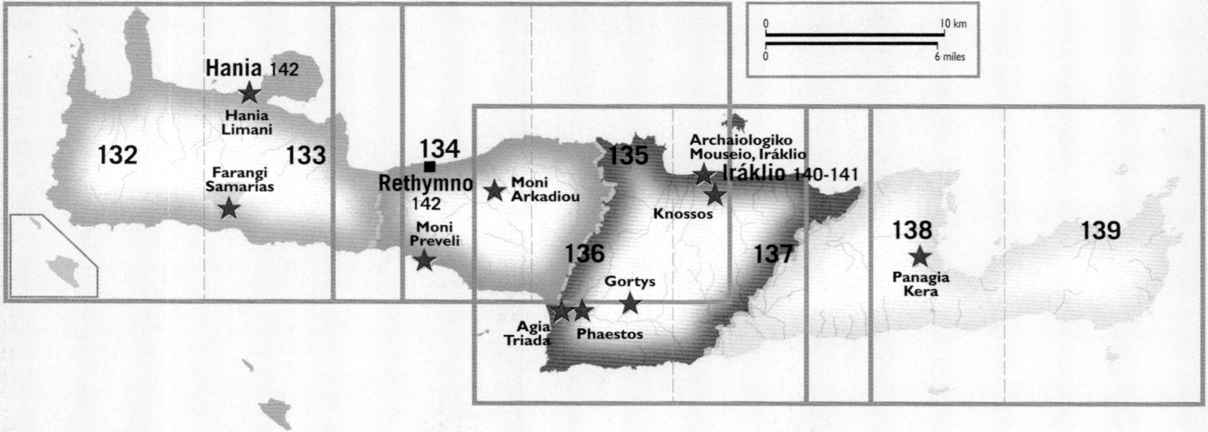

0 km 10
0 miles 6

**Best places to see**

★ Featured sight

■

| | Iráklio Province |
| | Lasithiou Province |
| | Rethymno Province |
| | Hania Province |

139

138
Panagia Kera

Archaiologiko
Mouseio, Iráklio
Iráklio 140–141

137

★ Knossos

135

★ Gortys

136 ★ Phaestos

★ Agia Triada

★ Moni Arkadiou

134
Rethymno 142
■
Moni Preveli ★

133

Hania 142 ★
Hania Limani

★ Farangi Samarias

132

Akr Spanda

A

1    2    3    4

Nisi Agria Gramvousa
Akr Vouxa

Nisi Gramvousa
O Gramvousa
Akr Tigani

Pondikonisi

Akr Skala

R o d o p o ú

748m ▲
Onihas

Kolpos
Kissamou

Rodopos □    **Moni Gonias**
**Kolimbari**

B

762m ▲
Geroskinos

**Maleme** □

**Falassarna** □
Akr Koutri

**Kissamos** □

Darmarohori □    Vlaheronitissa □
Drapanias □    Loutraki □

Limani □    Platanos □    Potamida □    Episkopi □    Zounaki □
Pervolakia □    Voukolies □    Vatolakkos □

C    Lousakies □    Horeftiana □    Deliana □    Pigi □    Skonizo □
Kalathenes □    Zimbragos □    Deres □    Langos □

O Sfinari    Sineniana □    Kakopetros □    Platanes □    1849m ▲    Langos □
Sfinari □    Melissia □    Plataniani
Kambos □    Kostogiannides □    Sasalos □    Pal Roumata □    Nea
Afrotolaki □    Rogdia □    Floria □    Sembronas □    Roumata □    Hosti □
Akr Karavoutas    Kefali □    Elos □    Aligi □    Spina □

D    Plokamiana □    Tzitzifia □    Ag Irini □
Moustakos □    Arhontiko □    Kandanos □
O Stomiou    Kalamios □    Sarakina □    Bambakados □    L
**Moni**    Agriles □    e
**Chrysoskalitissas** □    Kondokinigi □    Vlithias □    **Moni** □
Kamaria □
**Elafonisi** □    Ag Theodori    Spaniakos □    Azogires □    Koustogerako □
Prodromi □    **Sougia** □

E    Anidri □
Nisi Gavdopoula    Akr Krios    **Palaeochora** □    O Selino
Kastelli    Akr K

Akr Padouraki

F    *Gavdos*
Kastri □

**132**    1    Akr Tripiti    2    3    4

1　　　　2　　　　3　　　　4

Akr Drapano

Kokkino Horio

Drapanos

Kefalas

Likotinaria

Ormos
Almirou

Exopoli

Panormo

Skaleta

Angelliana

Prinos

Perama

Platanias

**Rethymno**

Ananepiskopi

Gerani

Prines

Kirianna

Mili

Ag Triada

Roupes

Kalandare

Mathes

Mouri

Dramia

Kato
Valsamonero

Somatas

Prasies

Kinigiana

Episkopi

Ag Andreas

Kavousi

★ **Moni
Arkadiou**

3m

Kournas

Patima

Armeni

Filakio

Selli

Argiroupoli

Roustika

Fotinos

Asigonia

Ano Malaki

Koumi

Geni

Marolou

Velonado

Karines

Ag Fotini

Thronos

Miriokefala

Arolithi
**1312m**
Krioneritis

Alones

Ag Ioannis

Koxare

Amari

Vistagi

Monastiraki

los

Atsipades

Mourne

Spili

Gerakari

Vizari

kiana

Skaloti

Kato
Rodakino

Sellia

Mariou

Frati

Kissos

Ano Meros

**Frangokastello**

O Plakia

**Plaklas**

Drimiskos

Kendrohori

Akr Kalogeros

Akr Kakomouri

Damnoni

Glannou

Akoumia
**1136m**
▲
Siderotas

Orne

Platis

**Moni Preveli**

**Preveli**

Melambes

**Agia Galini**

Ag Pavlos

Akr
Melissa

1　　　　2　　　　3　　　　4

## Map labels

**A**

**B**

Akr Korakias

**C**

Akr Stavros

O Fodele

Ag Pelagia

Akr Korakias

Akr Panagia

Kolpos
Irakliou

Ahlades

□ **Bali**

Sises

Ahlada

**Spilaio Tou**

**Melidoni**

Melidoni

*Koul o u k o n a s*

**Fodele**

Rogdia

**137**

Agia

Aloïdes

Marathos

**Iráklio**

*Geropotamos*

Ag Silas

Doxarou

Honos

Gazi

**D**

Garazo

Aidonohori

Kavrohori

**Knossos** ★

Veni

**Tilisos**

Kato Kalesa

Silamos

Ag Mamas

Axos

Gonies

1199m ▲
Voskero

Korfes

Voutes

Livadia

**Zoniana**

Stavrakia

Ag Sillas

Kounavi

*d* 1575m ▲
Sitaras

**Anogia**

Ag Mironas

**Pano
Arhanes**

**E**

Krousanas

*Giorfios*

2456m ■

**Óros Psiloreitis**

Fourfouras

Kato Asites

**Dafnes**

Venerato

**Prof Ilias**

Kerasia

Afgeniki

Kiparissos

Houdetsi

Nithafris

1920m ▲
Alikadam

Karkadiotissa

Pats

Apodoulou

Kamares

Ag Thomas

Platanos

Magarikari

**Zaros**

**Gergeri**

Megali Vrisi

Genna

Metaxohori

**F**

Ag Varvara

Ano Moulia

Larani

Melidohori

Tef

Klima

Moroni

Kato
Moulia

Kokkinos
Pirgos

Lagolio

Kissi

**136**

Inia

Valis

Ligortinos

Timbaki

**Vori**

Galia

**Gortys**

*(P s i l o r i t i s)*

**135**

A

Akr Stavros

Panormo □    ■ **Bali**    Akr Korakias    O Fodele    Ag Pelagia

Skaleta □    Ahlades □    **Spilaio Tou**    Sises    Ahlada

Angelliana □    **Melidoni** ■    **Fodele** ■

Prinos □    **Perama** □    □ Melidoni    Rogdia □

gi    Viranepiskopi □    □ Agia    Aloides □    Geropotamos    Marathos

Kirianna □    □ Ag Silas    Doxarou □

□ Roupes    Garazo □    Honos □    Aidonohori □

B

□ Kalandare    □ Veni    Kavrohori □

Kavousi □    □ Kinigiana    Ag Mamas □    □ Axos    **Tilisos** ■

ilakio    ★ **Moni**    Livadia □    Kato Kalesa    Korfes

**Arkadiou**    **Zoniana** □    **Anogia** ■    Gonies □    1199m

Ag Fotini □    □ Thronos    1575m    ▲ Voskero    Ag Mironas □

C

□ Vistagi    ▲ Sitaras    Krousonas □    **Dafnes** □

Amari □ □ Monastiraki    2456m    Kato Asites □    Venerato

e    □ Gerakari    Vizari □    **Óros Psiloreitis**    Kerasia □

issos    Ano Meros □    Fourfouras    Afgeniki □

□ Kendrohori    □ Nithafris    1920m    Ag Thomas □

6m    Apodoulou □    ▲ Alikadam    Ag Varvara □

erotas    **Melambes** □    Platanos □    Kamares □    Megali Vris □

D

   Magarikari □    **Zaros** □    **Gergeri** □    Ano Moulia □

Klima □    Kato Moulia □

**Agia Galini** ■    Lagolio □    Kissi □    Moroni □    Inia

Kokkinos Pirgos □    Timbaki □    **Vori** ■    Galia □    ★ **Gortys**    Valis

**Agia**    **Phaestos** ★    Ag Deka □

**Triada** ★    Ag Ioannis □    **Mires**    Geropotamos

E

Ormos    Kamilari □    Petrokefali □    Platanos □    Vagionia □

Mesaras    Kalamaki □    Pitsidia □    Sivas □    Alithini □    Plora □

Nisi Paximadia    Pombla □    Vasiliki □    Loukia □

Akr    **Matala** ■    Pigaidakia □    Koumasa □    f

Matala    Andiskari □    Krotos □    Kapetaniana □

Gerokambos □

F

□ Kali Limenes    Lendas □

Akr Lithino

Nisi Dragonada

Akr Sideros

Nisi Gianisada

Akr Mavro

**Vai**

*O Grandes*

**Moni Toplou**

*Akr
Faneromeni*

*Akr
Vamvakia*

*O Sitias*

*Nisi Grandes*

Lidia

**Sitia**

Angathia

*Akr Plaka*

**Palekastro**

Ag Fotia

*O Karoumbes*

**Mohlos**

Skopi

Piskokefalo

Tourloti

Exo Mouliana

Stavromenos

Mitato

Langada

Sfaka

*Orno*

1237m

Skordilo

Epano
Episkopi

▲
*Prinias*

803m

Sfakia

Askordalia

Dafni

Sikea

Praesos

Sitanos

**Zakros**

Hrisopigi

Vori

Kato Zákros

*Akr Zakros*

Orino

Handras

Lamnoni

Stavrohori

Ag Stefanos

Lithines

Ziros

Hametoulo

Xerokambos

**Makrygialos**

Ag Triada

Kalo Horio

*Nisi Kavalli*

Koutsouras

Mavros
Kolimbos

Goudouras

Atherinolakkos

*Akr Goudoura*

*Steno Koufonisi*

*Nisi Koufonisi*

# Iráklio

Koules Fortress

Venetiko
Limani

Agios Petrou
Dominikanon

Istoriko Mouseio
Kritis

Greco
Park

Agios Titos

Krini Morosini        Agios Markos

★ Archaiologiko Mouseio

Agia Ekaterini

Platia
Ag Ekaterinis

Platia
Eleftherias

DIKEOSSINIS

Platia Glanitson
Kornarou

Platia Halidon
Romanou

H TRIKOUPI

GEORGIOU PAPANDREOU

# Rethymno

- Fortetza
- Archaiologiko Mouseio
- Kentro Sigkronis Ekastikis Dimiorgias Rethimnis
- Temenos Neratze
- Mouseio Istorias Kai Laikis Technis

Venetiko Limani

Platia Georgiou
Platia P Vardogianni
Platia P Vardogianni
Platia T Martiron
Platia Iroon

Streets: KEFALOGIANNIDON, Makedonias, Himaras, Salaminos, Melissinou, Minoos, Kadamanthis, Paleologou, Soulou, Vernardou, Papamihelaki, Tsouderon, Tsagri, Arkadiou, ELEFTHERIOU VENIZELOU, Ethnikis, Ag Georgiou, Dimakopoulou, Ag Varvara, Gerakari, KOUNDOURIOTOU, Arkadiou, Sifi Vlastou, Syntagmatos, ICOUMENOU GAVRIL, Hexelii, PERIFERIAKI LEOFOROS, Metaxaki, Tsouli, Foka, P Koroneou, R Fereou, Filikon, Mavili, Piga, Patelarou, Nikiforou, Foka

# Hania

- Hania Limani ★
- Vizantino Mouseio
- Mouseio Nautiko
- Archaiologiko Mouseio
- Pal Dimotiki Agora

Venetiko Limani

Platia Talo
Platia Katehaki
Platia Merarhias
Platia Spantzias
Platia Athinagora
Platia S Venizelou
Platia Mahis Kritis
Platia 1866

Streets: Akti Kanari, Akti Tombazi, Akti Enosteos, Akti Koundourioti, Theotokopoulou Portou, Lithinon, Kanevaro, Kalergon, Sikaka, Zambeliou, Karaoli, Dimitriou, Pote, Sarpaki, Dikaioglanni, Vourdoumba, Melidoni, Episkopou, Minoa, Kiprou, Ioanninon, NIKIFOROU FOKA, Nikiforou Glanni, Isouutiron, HATZIMIHALI GIANARI, Khani, Koraka, SKALIDI, ZIMVRAKAKIDON, KIDONIAS, APOKORONOU PERIDI, TZANAKAKI, Youpodari, Stakion, Bonialis Pecule P, DIMOKRATIAS, H Trikoupi, KORAI, EL VENIZELOU, Iganinon, Mel Piga, Mel Merakaki, Patr, Gerassimou, Paschali Ger, Mitr Kiriliou, SELINOU, KISSAMOU, Pireos

# Notes

# Titles in the series

Algarve
Amsterdam
Andalucia
Athens
Australia
Austria
Barbados
Barcelona
Brittany
Budapest
California
Canada East
Canada West
China
Corfu
Costa Blanca
Costa Brava
Costa del Sol
Crete
Croatia
Cuba
Cyprus
Disneyland Resort Paris
Dominican Republic
Dubai
Dublin
Edinburgh
Egypt
England
Florence & Tuscany
Florida
French Riviera

Gran Canaria
Ibiza & Formentera
Iceland
Ireland
Italian Lakes
Italy
Lanzarote & Fuerteventura
London
Madeira
Madrid
Mallorca
Malta & Gozo
Menorca
Mexico
Naples & the Amalfi Coast
New York
New Zealand
Normandy
Orlando
Paris
Portugal
Prague
Provence & Cote d'Azur
Rhodes
Rome
Scotland
South Africa
Tenerife
Thailand
Tunisia
Venice